W9-BYR-921

Inferno

JULY 1943 – APRIL 1945

By

Eleanor H. Ayer

Academic Editor:

Dr. William L. Shulman

President, Association of Holocaust Organizations
Director, Holocaust Resource Center & Archives, New York

Series Advisor:

Dr. Michael Berenbaum

President & CEO of Survivors of the
Shoah Visual History Foundation, Los Angeles

Series Editor:

Lisa Clyde Nielsen

Advisory Board:

Dr. Minton Goldman, Associate Professor of Political Science,
Northeastern University, Boston

Kathryn Schindler, Teacher, Laguna Niguel Middle School, California;
multicultural and tolerance educator

Kathryn Greenberg, Educational and public-administration specialist,
Chicago Department of Public Health, Division of School Health

Rachel Kubersky, BA Library Education, MPH

Joachim Kalter, Holocaust survivor

Gloucester Library
P.O. Box 2380
Gloucester, VA 23061

Gloucester Library
P.O. Box
Gloucester, VA 23061

A BLACKBIRCH PRESS BOOK

WOODBRIDGE, CONNECTICUT

940.5318 Aye

Acknowledgments

Many people have given generously of their time and knowledge during the development of this series. We would like to thank the following people in particular: Genya Markon, and the staff at the United States Holocaust Memorial Museum Photo Archives—Leslie Swift, Sharon Muller, Alex Rossino, and Teresa Pollin—for their talented guidance; and Dr. Michael Berenbaum, currently President and CEO of the Survivors of the Shoah Visual History Foundation and formerly Director of the Research Institute at the U.S. Holocaust Memorial Museum, for his valuable editorial input and his enthusiastic support of our efforts.

Dr. William L. Shulman, President of the Association of Holocaust Organizations and the Holocaust Resource Center & Archives at Queensborough Community College, merits special mention. As the series academic editor—as well as the compiler of Books 7 and 8—Dr. Shulman's guidance, insight, and dedication went far beyond the call of duty. His deep and thorough knowledge of the subject gave us all the critical perspective we needed to make this series a reality.

Published by Blackbirch Press, Inc.
260 Amity Road
Woodbridge, CT 06525

web site: http://www.blackbirch.com
e-mail: staff@blackbirch.com

©1998 Blackbirch Press, Inc.
First Edition

All rights reserved. No part of this book may be reproduced in any form without permission in writing from Blackbirch Press, Inc., except by a reviewer.

Printed in the United States of America

10 9 8 7 6 5 4 3 2 1

Cover: Children peer out from behind the barbed wire at Auschwitz (State Archives of the Russian Federation, courtesy of USHMM Photo Archives).

Library of Congress Cataloging-in-Publication Data

Ayer, Eleanor.
Inferno, June 1943 to May 1945 / by Eleanor H. Ayer
p. cm. — (Holocaust)
Includes bibliographical references and index.
ISBN 1-56711-205-6 (alk. paper)
1. Holocaust, Jewish (1939–1945)—Juvenile literature. 2. Jewish children in the Holocaust—Juvenile literature. I. Title. II. Series: Holocaust (Woodbridge, Conn.)
D804.34.A94 1998
940.53'18—dc21 96-48528
CIP
AC

CONTENTS

Preface 4

Foreword by Dr. Michael Berenbaum 5

INTRODUCTION
Dark Years 9

1 JULY–SEPTEMBER 1943
"They Weren't Humans" 15

2 OCTOBER 1943–MARCH 1944
"We Have No Time" 25

3 MARCH–JUNE 1944
"Butterflies Don't Live Here in the Ghetto" 35

4 JUNE–SEPTEMBER 1944
"We Didn't Know" 43

5 SEPTEMBER 1944–JANUARY 1945
"We Had Been Counted" 53

6 FEBRUARY–APRIL 1945
"Nothing but Bread" 63

Chronology of the Holocaust: 1933-1945 73
Glossary 74
Source Notes 76
Bibliography 78
Further Reading 78
Index 79

Preface

At the United States Holocaust Memorial Museum in Washington, D.C., a poignant documentary explores antisemitism and its role in the Holocaust. The film ends with these words:

THIS IS WHERE PREJUDICE CAN LEAD.

That somber warning has guided our work on this series.

The task of creating a series of books on the Holocaust seemed, at first, straightforward enough: We would develop an in-depth account of one of the most complex and compelling periods in human history.

But it quickly became clear to us that, on an emotional level, this series would not be straightforward at all. Indeed, the more work we did, the more we realized just how this subject wraps itself around everyone it touches. As we discussed content with our authors and advisors and began to select photographs and other documents for reproduction, several unanticipated and complicated issues arose.

The first major issue was pivotal, in that our decision would guide the content of the books: How should we choose to define the very term *Holocaust?* Many scholars of the Holocaust believe that the term should be used exclusively in reference to the approximately 6 million European Jews who were murdered by Nazis and their collaborators between 1933 and 1945. This is because no other group was singled out so systematically and relentlessly for genocide. Should the perhaps 4 million non-Jewish victims of the period—the Soviet prisoners of war, Romani (Gypsies), Jehovah's Witnesses, German and Austrian male homosexuals, and other groups—be discussed on the same level as the Jews? Ultimately—in philosophical agreement with the U.S. Holocaust Memorial Museum—we decided to focus our discussion primarily on the Jews but also to report the experiences of other victims.

Our second major decision had to do with how to present the material. How explicit should the books be in their written descriptions and photographic records of what was done to the victims? Perhaps never before have the brutalities of war and the consequences of prejudice and hatred been so extensively chronicled; perhaps never so eloquently and, at the same time, in such painful detail.

On this issue, we decided we would chronicle what happened, but try not to shock or horrify. Learning about the Holocaust should be disturbing—but there is a delicate line between informative realism and sensationalism. The most brutal accounts and documentation of the Holocaust can be found in many other sources; we believe that in our series, much of this story will be revealed through the powerful and moving images we have selected.

Yet another difficult issue was raised by our educational advisors: Was the Holocaust truly a singular historical event, uniquely qualified for such detailed study as is provided in this series? That it was an extraordinary period in history, there can be no denial—despite some misguided people's efforts to the contrary. Certainly, never before had an entire nation organized its power and mobilized itself so efficiently for the sole purpose of destroying human life. Yet the Holocaust was not unique in terms of the number of people murdered; nor was it unique in the brutality of the hatred on which it fed.

A subject such as this raises many questions. How could the Holocaust have happened? Could it have been prevented? How can we keep this from happening again? We have done our best to explore the questions we feel are most central. Ultimately, however, the most compelling questions to emerge from learning about the Holocaust are for each individual reader to answer.

Foreword

There is a paradox in the study of the Holocaust: The more distant we are from the Event, the more interest seems to grow. In the immediate aftermath of the Holocaust, horrific images were played in movie theaters on newsreels, which was how people saw the news in an era before television. Broadcasting on CBS radio, famed newscaster Edward R. Murrow said:

> *Permit me to tell you what you would have seen and heard had you been with me on Thursday. It will not be pleasant listening. If you are at lunch or have no appetite to hear of what Germans have done, now is a good time to turn off your radio, for I propose to tell you of Buchenwald.*

Murrow described the sights and sounds of what he had experienced in the immediate aftermath of liberation, and his audience was appropriately horrified. Action was required, trials were soon held—an accounting for a deed that was beyond human comprehension, a crime beyond a name, that we now call the "Holocaust."

Shortly thereafter, interest waned. Other topics of the era took center stage—the Cold War, the Berlin blockade, the Korean War—and it seemed for a time that the Holocaust would be forgotten. In retrospect, we can surmise that the silence was a necessary response to such catastrophe. Distance was needed before we could look back and muster enough courage to confront an event so terrible.

No one could have imagined that, half a century after the Holocaust, museums such as the United States Holocaust Memorial Museum would be built and would attract millions of visitors each year. No one, too, would have guessed that films such as *Schindler's List* would be seen by tens of millions of people throughout the world. No one could have foreseen that thousands of books would be published on the subject and courses in schools all over the world would be taught—that interest in this horrible chapter of history would intensify rather than recede with the passage of time.

Why study the Holocaust?

The answer is simple: Because it happened!

An event of such magnitude, a state-sponsored annihilation of an entire people—men, women, and children—must be confronted. Some people have portrayed the Holocaust as an aberration, a world apart from the ordinary world in which we dwell. Even the most eloquent of survivors, Elie Wiesel, calls it the "Kingdom of Night." Yet, to me the Holocaust is not an aberration, but an expression in the extreme of a common thread that runs through our civilization. And thus, not to confront the Event is not to probe the deep darkness that is possible within our world.

Because it happened, we must seek to understand the anguish of the victims—the men, women, and children who faced death and had impossible choices to make, and who could do so little to determine their fate. And we must seek to understand the neutrality and indifference of the bystanders around the world; and what caused the Allies—who were fighting a full-scale world war against the Germans and other Axis powers—to fail to address the "second war," the war against the Jews.

We must also seek to understand the all-too-few non-Jewish heroes of the Holocaust—the men, women, and children who opened their homes and their hearts and provided a haven for the victims; a place to sleep, a crust of bread, a kind word, a hiding place. What makes such goodness possible? Why were they immune to the infection of evil?

We must understand that the Holocaust did not begin with mass killing. Age-old prejudice led to discrimination, discrimination led to persecution, persecution to incarceration, incarceration to annihilation. And mass murder, which culminated with the killing of approximately 6 million Jews, did not begin with the Jews—nor did it encompass only the Jews. The state-sponsored murder of the physically and mentally disabled was a precursor to the Holocaust. It was in that killing process that gas chambers and crematoria were developed and refined, and the staff of the death camps were trained. Romani (commonly but incorrectly referred to as Gypsies) were killed alongside the Jews. Jehovah's Witnesses, German and Austrian male homosexuals, political prisoners and dissidents were also incarcerated in concentration camps, where many were murdered. Gentile and Jewish Poles were subjected to decimation and destruction of their national identity. Though many Jews suffered alone, abandoned and forgotten by the world, they were not the only ones to die.

The study of the Holocaust is not easy. We are often unclear about whose history is being taught: German history, Jewish history, American history, European history. And to understand it, we need to understand more than history. Other disciplines are essential, such as psychology and sociology, political science, philosophy and theology, and, most especially, ethics. When we study the Holocaust, we are forced to face evil, to confront experiences that are horrific and destructive. And even despite the tools of all these disciplines, we still may not understand. Comprehension may elude us.

With the renewed interest in the Holocaust—especially in North America—we have seen that the study of all these deaths is actually in the service of life; the study of evil actually strengthens decency and goodness. For us as free citizens, confronting this European event brings us a new recognition of the principles of constitutional democracy: a belief in equality and equal justice under law; a commitment to pluralism and toleration; a determination to restrain government by checks and balances and by the constitutional protection of "inalienable rights"; and a struggle for human rights as a core value.

The Holocaust shatters the myth of innocence and, at the same time, has implications for the exercise of power. Those who wrestle with its darkness know it can happen again—even in the most advanced, most cultured, most "civilized" of societies. But, if we are faithful to the best of human values, the most sterling of our traditions, then we can have confidence that it "won't happen here." These truths are not self-evident; they are precarious and, therefore, even more precious.

The Holocaust has implications for us as individuals. As we read these books, we can't help but ask ourselves, "What would I have done?" "If I were a Jew, would I have had the courage to resist—spiritually or militarily—and when?" "Would I have had the wisdom and the ability to flee to a place that offered a haven?" "Do I have a friend who would offer me a place of shelter, a piece of bread, a moment of refuge?" "What could I have done to protect my family, to preserve my life?"

We can't offer easy answers because the options were few, the pressures extreme, the conditions unbearable, and the stakes ultimate—life or death.

We may also ask ourselves even more difficult questions: "What prejudices do I have?" "Do I treat all people with full human dignity?" "Am I willing to discriminate against some, to scapegoat others?" "Am I certain—truly certain—that I could not be a killer? That I would not submit to the pressures of conformity and participate in horrible deeds or, worse yet, embrace a belief that makes me certain—absolutely certain—that I am right and the others are wrong? That my cause is just and the other is an enemy who threatens me, who must be eliminated?" These are questions you will ask as you read these books—ask, but not answer.

Perhaps, in truth, the more intensely you read these books, the less certainty you will have in offering your personal answer. Premature answers are often immature answers. Good questions invite one to struggle with basic values.

The central theme of the story of the Holocaust is not regeneration and rebirth, goodness or resistance, liberation or justice, but, rather, death and destruction, dehumanization and devastation, and above all, loss.

The killers were "civilized" men and women of an advanced culture. They were both ordinary and extraordinary, a true cross-section of the men and women of Germany, its allies, and their collaborators, as well as the best and the brightest. In these volumes, those deeds will be seen, as will the evolution of policy, the expansion of the power of the state, and technological and scientific murders unchecked by moral, social, religious, or political constraints. Whether restricted to the past or a harbinger of the future, the killers demonstrated that systematic mass destruction is possible. Under contemporary conditions, the execution of such a policy would only be easier.

The Holocaust transforms our understanding. It shatters faith—religious faith in God and secular faith in human goodness. Its truth has been told not to provide answers, but to raise questions. To live conscientiously in its aftermath, one must confront the reality of radical evil and its past triumphs. At the same time, we must fight against that evil and its potential triumphs in the future.

The call from the victims—from the world of the dead—is to remember. From the survivors, initial silence has given way to testimony. The burden of memory has been transmitted and thus shared. From scholars, philosophers, poets, and artists—those who were there and those who were not—we hear the urgency of memory, its agony and anguish, its meaning and the absence of meaning. To live in our age, one must face the void.

Israel Ba'al Shem Tov, the founder of Hasidism, once said:

In forgetfulness is the root of exile.
In remembrance, the seed of
redemption.

His fears of forgetting, we understand all too well.

Whether we can share his hope of remembrance is uncertain.

Still, it is up to us to create that hope.

Michael Berenbaum
Survivors of the Shoah
Visual History Foundation
Los Angeles, California

I N T R O D U C T I O N

Dark Years

By May 1943, World War II had been raging in Europe for nearly four years. Germany's leader, Adolf Hitler, whose dreams of power and glory had fueled that war, now controlled much of Europe. His armies had conquered an area from the Scandinavian countries in the north, to Greece and Italy in the south, and from France into the western part of what was then the Soviet Union.

Throughout the vast empire called the Third Reich, Hitler and the Nazis targeted groups of innocent people for persecution and death. Their victims included Jews, Romani (commonly but incorrectly called Gypsies), male homosexuals, Jehovah's Witnesses, Poles, political enemies, and the physically and mentally handicapped. The Nazis called some of these people *Untermenschen*, or "subhumans."

Prisoners of Buchenwald peer out from their bunks in the spring of 1945.

Louis Arzt, a 12-year-old Jehovah's Witness, was taken from his home in France and shipped to a concentration camp in Germany—all because at school he refused to say "Heil Hitler!" Saying those words would have shown that Arzt honored Adolf Hitler as the supreme leader. His religious training did not allow him to praise Hitler, or anyone, above Jehovah. And so Arzt was beaten, harassed, and told, "Think of your mother. She would be happy to see you. All you need to do is to say 'Heil Hitler!' and you can get on the train [to go home]." Arzt refused.

The group for whom Hitler and his supporters reserved their greatest hatred—and on whom they inflicted the most cruelty—was the Jews. Hitler called his plan for the Jews the "Final Solution." It proposed genocide—the murder of an entire racial, ethnic, or large social group—in this case, the Jews.

Hitler's Nazi Party had grown from an upstart political group in the 1920s into an awesome force that included the mighty SS—the *Schutzstaffel* or protection squad—the most powerful organization in the Third Reich.

The most-feared branch of the SS was the Gestapo—the Nazi secret police, whose job it was to search out and arrest those whom the Nazis labeled *Untermenschen*. Heinrich Himmler, one of the highest-ranking Nazis in wartime Germany, was chief of the SS and head of the Gestapo.

Another SS branch, the Death's Head Brigade, operated hundreds of concentration (labor) camps across the Reich. There, millions of people perished as the result of torture, starvation, and disease. The Death's Head Brigade also ran six extermination centers in Poland—death camps, terrifying killing centers where millions more people were murdered outright. The SS was also responsible for establishing ghettos in sections of major cities. Jews were rounded up and forced to live there in conditions of severe overcrowding, filth, and starvation.

Himmler was ultimately given the responsibility for carrying out Hitler's Final Solution, which very nearly was achieved during the Holocaust. The word *holocaust* generally means a

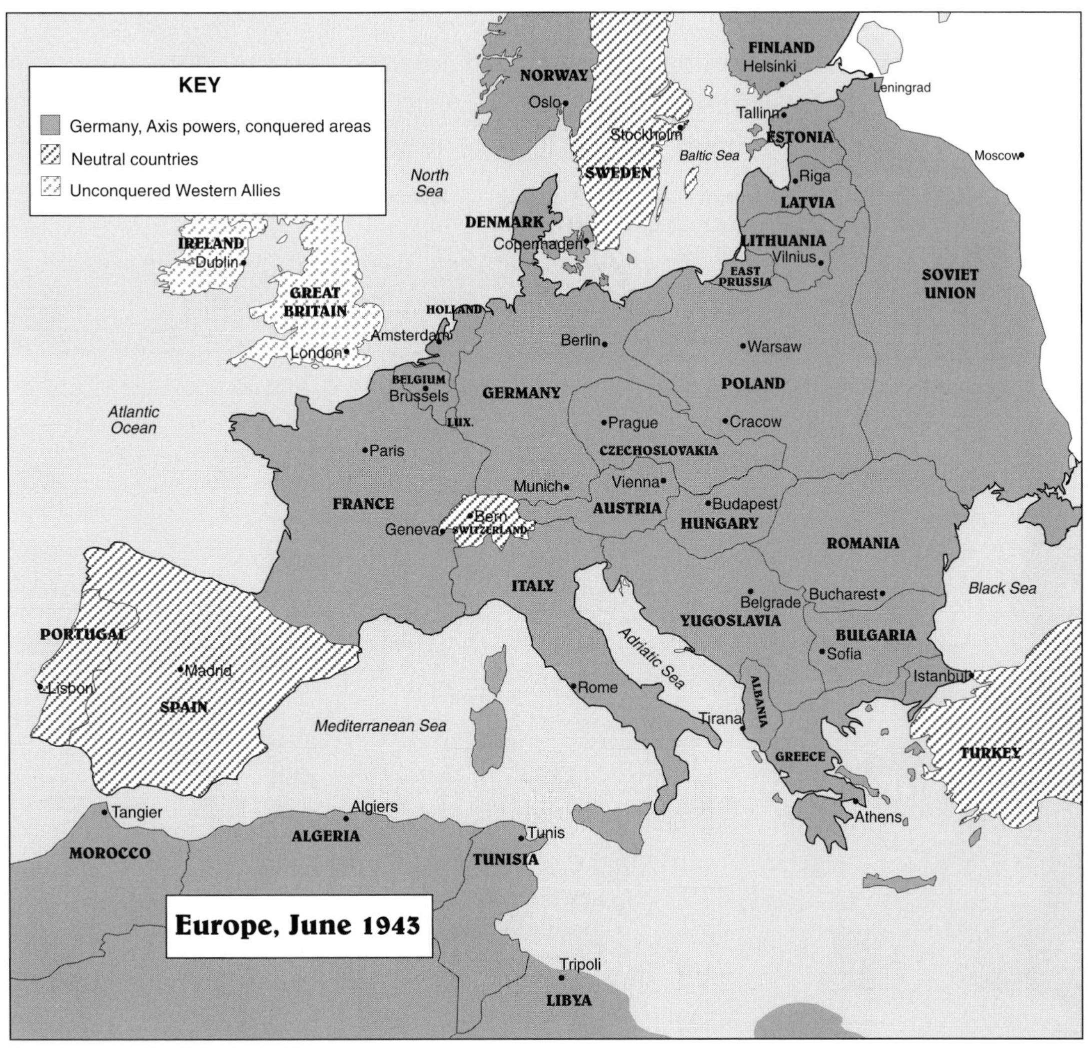

"destruction of life by fire." But, when the word is spelled with a capital *H*, it refers to that period in history from 1933 to 1945 when the Nazis, under Adolf Hitler, systematically persecuted and killed millions of Jews and other people. However, most historians consider the Holocaust a particularly Jewish tragedy because Jews were the group that was most methodically and systematically singled out for death.

Why was the Holocaust allowed to happen? Why didn't someone do something to stop the persecution and murders of so many people? There are many reasons, and none of them is

Deportations increased dramatically from 1943 to 1945. Here, residents of the ghetto in Cracow, Poland, are deported to camps in March 1943.

simple or absolute. Many Europeans, especially Germans, chose to ignore the situation rather than protest the Nazis' persecution of their neighbors. The majority of citizens didn't want to endanger their own lives or put their families at risk. The plight of the Jews was somebody else's problem, most believed.

Furthermore, some countries had long been antisemitic. In some places, persecution of Jews was actively supported by the local populace.

Few churches or religious leaders took a stand against Hitler; in fact, many supported him. Even foreign governments and world leaders, including the United States under President Franklin D. Roosevelt, did little or nothing to help the Jews. Economic depression and high unemployment made the problems of the Jews in Europe seem less important than the poverty that faced many Americans at home.

Why didn't Jews simply leave Europe? Many countries had a quota system, which allowed only a certain number of Jews to enter. Government leaders worried that immigrants would take jobs away from citizens or would become welfare problems themselves. But had these countries increased their quotas or done away with the system altogether, hundreds of thousands of lives would likely have been saved.

Because the Final Solution affected Jews living, dead, and not yet born, the Holocaust is considered the ultimate crime against Jewry in modern times. In the words of Jewish Holocaust survivor Elie Wiesel, "Not all of the victims were Jewish, but all of the Jews were victims."

The Holocaust was one of the darkest eras in history. Even today, more than half a century later, it is impossible to fully comprehend the events that took place during those years. Because the entire era was filled with cruelty and inhumanity, it is difficult to single out one period as being worse than the rest. The months from June 1943 until the liberation of the camps in April and May 1945, however, were particularly brutal. This tragic period marked the peak of the Final Solution.

"They Weren't Humans"

Jewish schoolgirl Aviva Unger was 12 years old when she was shipped with her mother to Poland's Warsaw ghetto. Shortly after they arrived, her mother had a stroke that left her partially paralyzed. It was not long before the Nazis shot her.

With the help of a Gentile (non-Jewish) friend, Unger escaped from the ghetto by crawling through Warsaw's sewer system. She was taken to a Catholic convent, where she lived with nuns until Easter of 1943. While she was riding a streetcar one day, a Jewish spy for the Gestapo recognized Unger as a Jew and turned her in. "I spent four days in the Gestapo [headquarters]," she later remembered, where "they hit and kicked me ceaselessly to get information out of me. . . . I wasn't yet quite 15. They weren't humans, those Gestapo."

Lost and abandoned bundles lie strewn on a street in Cracow, Poland, after Jews from the ghetto were deported in the spring of 1943.

A priest from the convent saved Unger by swearing that her family was Catholic. Reluctantly, the Gestapo released her. Though she was free, Unger still faced a frightening future. At any moment she might be snared again, and this time she might not find help. Jews across Europe shared her fear during this period, when the Nazis shipped millions of people to death and concentration camps.

"Savagery"

In July 1942, Heinrich Himmler ordered the liquidation, or removal, of people from the Jewish ghettos. By the spring of 1943, however, the task was still far from complete. In June of that year, Himmler demanded that all Jews living in the ghettos of the German-occupied parts of Poland and the Soviet Union be deported—sent away—at once. He ordered that those people be shipped to camps in the east, where they would be killed.

In the smaller communities of eastern Poland, the Nazis did not even bother deporting victims to death camps. They simply herded them into nearby forests or gravel pits and shot them, throwing their bodies into mass graves. Martin Gilbert, a historian, wrote: ". . . Executions were carried out with savagery and sadism, a crying child often being seized from its mother's arms and shot in front of her. . . ."

Heinrich Himmler (left) was responsible for ordering and overseeing the liquidation of all Jewish ghettos. Here, he dines with a fellow Nazi, Hans Frank.

Rumors of this savagery spread, often through the Jewish children who helped smuggle guns and goods into the ghetto. Reaction to Nazi atrocities sparked resistance and uprising within some ghettos. On July 24, 1943, in Vilnius, the capital of Lithuania—then part of the Soviet Union—21 Jewish resisters from a ghetto of 20,000 tried to escape and make contact with Soviet partisans. (Partisans were independent fighters whose goal was to harass German troops and upset Nazi actions.)

Nine of the 21 escapees were killed. The remainder found shelter in the forest and joined the Soviet partisans in disrupting German military communications and delivery of supplies to the front lines of battle.

In the Bialystok ghetto of northeastern Poland, a revolt began on August 15, when Germans ordered the remaining 40,000 to 45,000 residents deported to death camps. It took German artillery and tanks to stop the uprising. Said Haika Grossman, the leader of the revolt: "We knew that we would be the first to fall. . . . But the masses were behind us. If the barrier was opened, thousands would flee. . . ."

The Bialystok revolt failed, however, and most of the fighters died. Those caught were lined up against a wall and shot. The few rebels who managed to survive fled to the woods to join the partisans.

Major Concentration and Extermination Camps

The Death Camps

The Nazis' six extermination camps were all located in German-occupied Poland, because the greatest concentration of European Jews was to be found there. These death camps differed from concentration camps in that their sole function was to kill people. Victims were sent there to die, not to work. Like the concentration camps, the death camps were run by the SS.

The largest camp was in southwestern Poland, at Auschwitz. Auschwitz I was the concentration camp. The outright killings took place in Auschwitz II, known as Birkenau. At Auschwitz III,

The "Angel of Death"

In addition to conducting at least 74 "selection" sessions at the Auschwitz complex between May 1943 and November 1944—sessions in which he chose which people would live and which would die—Dr. Josef Mengele performed inhuman medical experiments on the inmates. His goal was to produce a race of perfect "Aryans." Nazi hunter Simon Wiesenthal wrote that Mengele believed that "human beings had pedigrees, like dogs. He was convinced of his mission to breed a super-race of blue-eyed, blond 'Nordic' people, and of his duty to kill 'biologically inferior specimens.'"

To produce his "perfect race," Mengele experimented on victims both dead and alive. Twins, dwarfs, and those with physical abnormalities especially interested him. Of the 3,000 twins who endured his sadistic treatment, only 157 survived. Two of those were Irene Hizme and her brother, Rene Slotkin. Irene later wrote:

> *[He] was a doctor. I trusted him. The first time, he took blood from my neck. It was very scary and very painful. But I didn't dare make a sound. If I did, I knew it would be worse. He gave me shots in my back and in my arm, and X-rays. Each time I left his laboratory, I was sick, very sick.*

At the end of the war, Mengele escaped to South America, where he lived in Brazil, Argentina, and Paraguay as one of the most wanted criminals of World War II. In 1985, family and friends at last confessed that he had drowned in 1979 in Brazil. Examination of the human remains buried in Paraguay confirmed that they were those of the "Angel of Death."

Buna-Monowitz, inmates were worked as slaves at hard labor, many of them in ironworks, until they died from exhaustion. From 1942 to its liberation day in 1945, from 1¼ million to 1½ million people were murdered at the Auschwitz complex.

The first extermination camp was built at Chelmno, in west-central occupied Poland. There, amid great secrecy, 300,000 to 310,000 people were murdered. Nearly all of the victims were Jews, but non-Jewish Poles, Soviet prisoners of war, Romani, and 88 children from the village of Lidice were also killed. At Chelmno, victims were loaded into large vans that were then filled with carbon monoxide, killing everyone inside. The bodies were taken to a nearby forest and burned. Only three or four people are known to have survived Chelmno.

Located in east-central Poland, not far from the River Bug, were three killing centers: Belzec, Majdanek, and Sobibór. At these camps, between 1942 and 1944, more than 1 million people perished.

Belzec had the capacity to kill 15,000 a day. Although it operated for only nine months, some 600,000 people died there. Only two survivors are known.

North of Belzec was Majdanek, located in the suburbs of Lublin, one of Poland's larger cities. "At Majdanek," wrote historian Konnilyn Feig, "nothing was wasted, everything was salvaged—ashes [from the burned bodies], gold fillings, bones, clothes, wooden arms, legs, and crutches, toothpaste, nail files, children's toys. . . ." The salvaged items were returned to Germany to be distributed to the people or used in the manufacture of products useful to the Reich. Among the most stirring reminders of mass murder, discovered when the camp was liberated in 1945, was a huge mound of shoes—some 500,000 of them—taken from the hundreds of thousands of victims who went to their deaths at Majdanek.

Sobibór, at the northernmost end of the chain of camps, sits today on a narrow road, marked by a stone monument that reads: AT THIS PLACE, 250,000 RUSSIAN, POLISH, JEWISH, AND ROMANI PRISONERS WERE MURDERED. The count may actually have been higher; exact figures from the death and concentration camps

A View of the Concentration Camps

By April 1944, the Nazis' concentration camp system had 20 main camps. There were also six death camps in German-occupied Poland. Attached to most of the 20 main camps were satellite camps that numbered nearly 500. The largest concentration camps were:

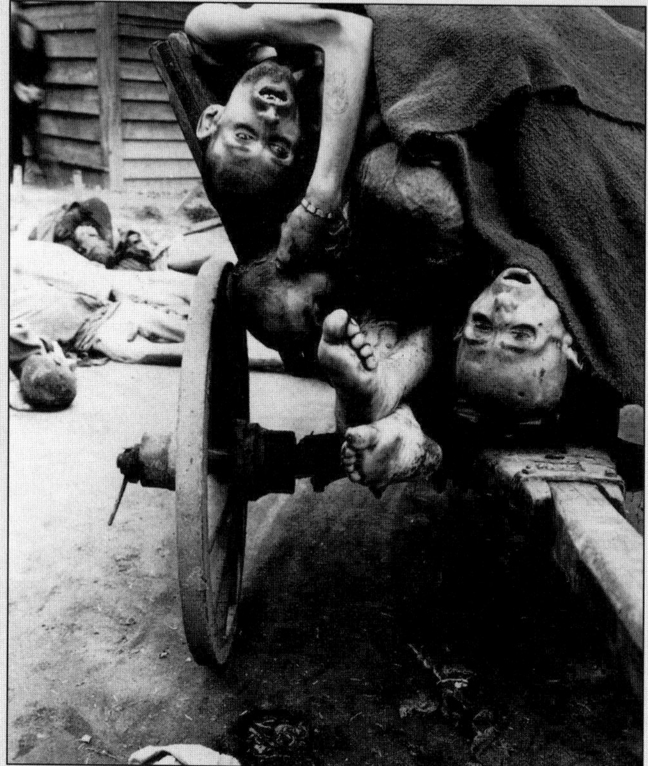

Gusen

- **Dachau (Germany):** Opened March 1933, less than two months after Hitler took power; liberated by American troops on April 29, 1945. What the Nazis used as a model for other camps is now open to the public as a memorial and museum.
- **Sachsenhausen (Germany):** Opened September 1936; liberated by Soviet troops on April 22, 1945. Located in the town of Oranienburg, where a few camp buildings still stand.
- **Buchenwald (Germany):** Opened July 1937; liberated by American troops on April 11, 1945. Today's Buchenwald National Memorial is divided into two parts: the old camp grounds and a monument park.
- **Flossenburg (Germany):** Opened May 1938; liberated by the Americans on April 23, 1945. Monuments, barbed wire, guardhouses, the gas chamber, and a crematorium still stand.
- **Mauthausen/Gusen (Austria):** Opened August 1938; liberated by the Americans on May 8, 1945. The site is now a historic monument and houses a museum.
- **Ravensbrück (Germany):** Opened May 1939; liberated by the Soviets on April 30, 1945. The women's camp, where approximately 92,000 women and children died, is today a National Memorial and Commemoration, designed as a lasting monument to the camp's victims.
- **Stutthof (occupied Poland):** Opened September 1939; liberated by the Soviets May 9, 1945. The crematorium, gas chamber, and many other buildings are open to the public.

■ **Neuengamme (Germany):** Opened June 1940; liberated by the British on May 3, 1945. The original camp site is a prison today. Around the grounds are a memorial and park.

■ **Gross Rosen (Germany):** Opened August 1940; liberated by the Soviets in February 1945. This was the center of Hitler's euthanasia or "mercy killing" program.

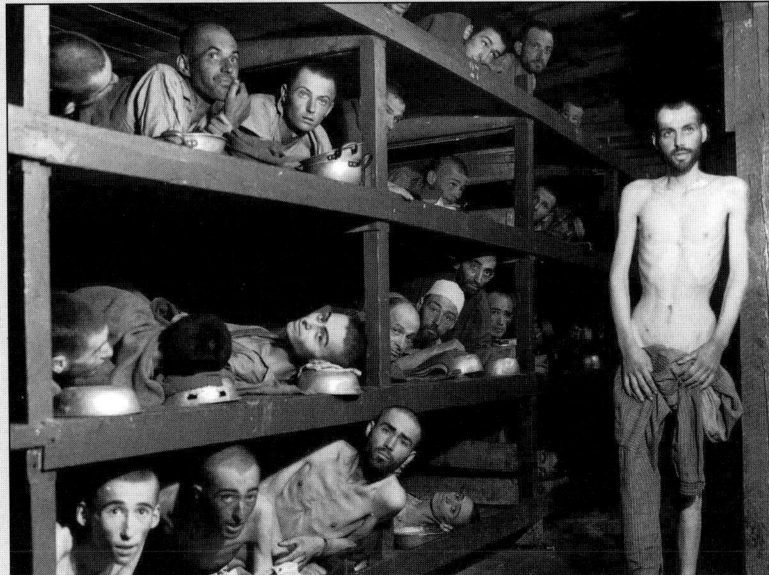

Buchenwald

■ **Natzweiler (occupied France):** Opened May 1941; evacuated by the Nazis in September 1944. The camp has been preserved as a memorial and museum.

■ **Theresienstadt (occupied Czechoslovakia):** Opened November 1941; liberated by the Soviets on May 8, 1945. It was located in the town of Terezin, which today houses a large military barracks.

Dachau

■ **Bergen-Belsen (Germany):** Opened April 1943; liberated by the British on April 15, 1945. Today, the site is a graveyard. Nothing remains of the original camp.

■ **Mittelbau Dora (Germany):** Opened September 1943; evacuated on April 5, 1945. Located in the town of Nordhausen, this was the site of the Nazis' rocket factory. Tunnels dug into the mountains for the factories are still in use by the government today.

will never be known. Although the Germans were meticulous record-keepers, the numbers of victims were too staggering to record an accurate count. Sobibór was a small camp, with only 20 barracks. But it didn't need more—most of its prisoners never even spent the night; they were murdered within hours of arriving.

The sixth death camp was Treblinka, in north-central Poland. Among the victims there was a child who had been separated from his parents when they were deported from the Warsaw ghetto in 1943. When the boy arrived at Treblinka, he spotted his father and ran into his arms. "They took me away in a train," the boy explained. "I was very thirsty and a little afraid. And now I have found you again. I knew I would!"

Danish fishermen ferry a boatload of Jews to safety in the neutral country of Sweden, 1943.

Just then a guard approached and told the child that he must go to take a shower. When the boy protested, the guard ordered his father to make him behave. "Go, go, I'll see you in a minute," his father insisted. The father knew, however, that Treblinka's showers released not water but a poisonous gas that killed everyone within minutes. The father had no choice but to send the child off to what would surely be his death. The boy was one of approximately 900,000 Jews who were killed at Treblinka during its operation.

The little boy's body was one of many thousands. They were becoming a big problem for the SS. As more and more people were murdered, finding enough burial space became difficult. Rather than try to find additional space, SS leader Heinrich Himmler decided that camp inmates themselves should perform the terrible task of digging up the bodies already buried and burn them.

Salvation of the Danish Jews

By September 1943, approximately 8,000 Jews living in German-occupied Denmark had been singled out for death. With the deportation set for early October, Danish resistance workers went into action. "Finding Jews, bringing them to the harbor, and organizing and protecting their embarkation became our most important tasks during the following weeks," recalled Jørgen Kieler, a student organizer of the Danish resistance movement. Nearly overnight, the workers gathered every available boat and boatman in Denmark and issued instructions for transporting Jews across the narrow waterway into Sweden, which was a neutral country in the war and thus a safe destination.

The Danes rescued more than 7,200 Jews, and most of them survived. Approximately 60 died during the war. Kieler credited the Jews with giving the Danish people the inspiration to do what was needed—help. "Jews don't owe us gratitude," he said years later. "Rather, we owe each other mutual friendship."

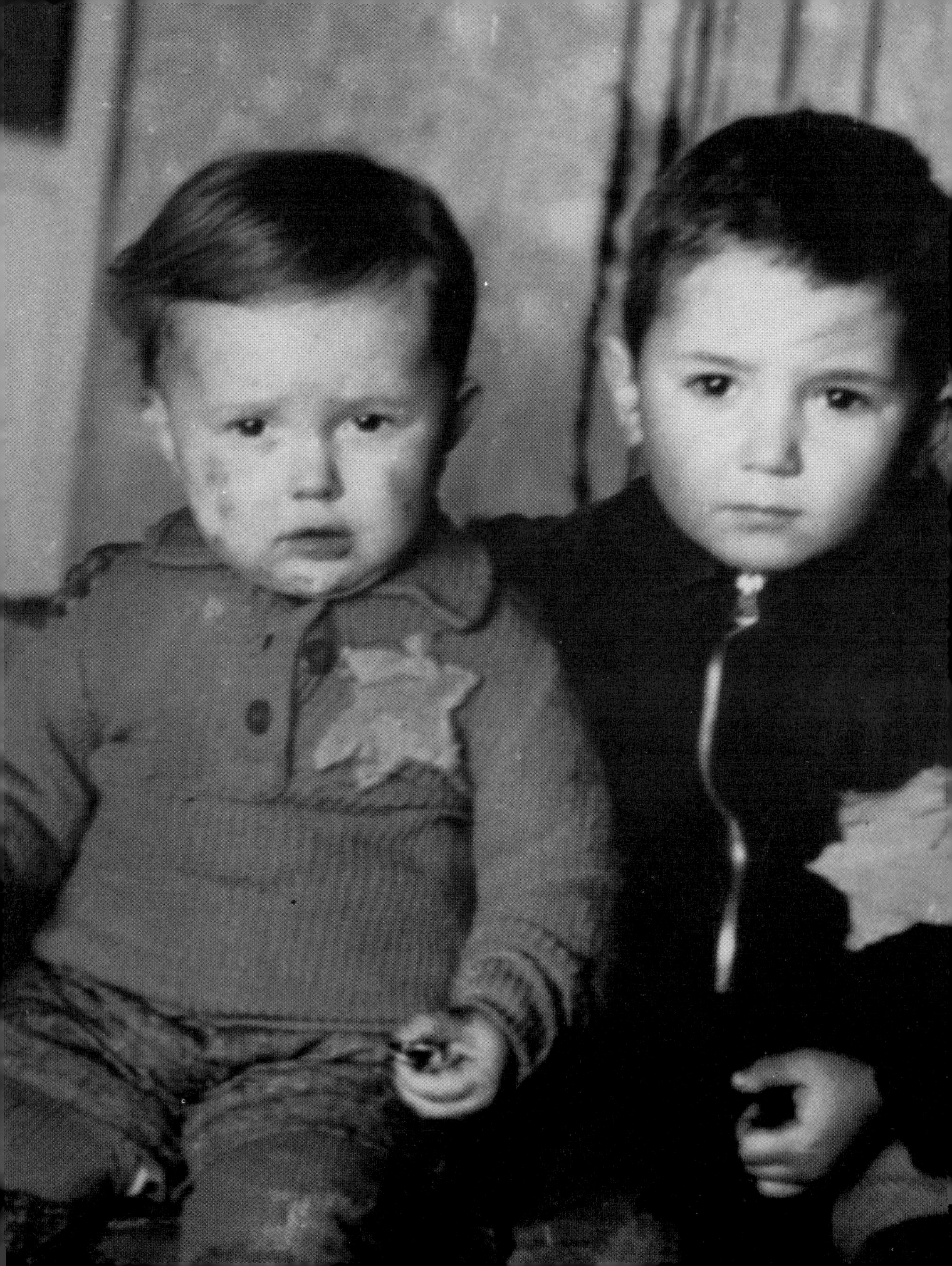

"We Have No Time"

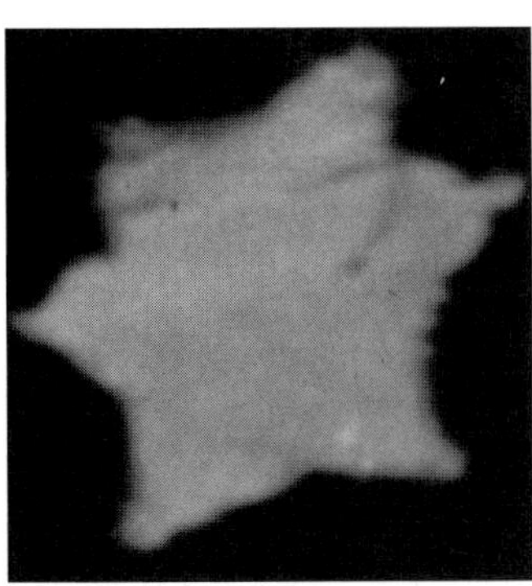

Tomasz (Toivi) Blatt was 16 years old when he was deported from Izbica, Poland, to the Sobibór extermination camp. There, on October 14, 1943, Tomasz became one of 600 prisoners who made a daring break for freedom.

The revolt began about 4:00 P.M. At first, everything went as scheduled. The plan was to have selected prisoners overcome the SS guards with homemade weapons, while the rest of the prisoners formed into orderly lines and marched through the main gate. By using this exit, they hoped to escape suspicion and to avoid the land mines that surrounded the rest of the camp. Soon, however, chaos erupted and prisoners began running frantically toward the barbed wire fence. Tomasz recalled the panic:

Avram Rosenthal (5 years old) and his brother Emmanuel (2 years old) endured the harsh life of the Kovno ghetto before being deported to Majdanek in March 1944, where they were murdered.

> *They weren't about to wait in line; there were machine guns shooting at us. They climbed on the fence and just as I was halfway through, it collapsed, trapping me underneath. This saved me. The first [prisoners] through hit mines. When most were through, I slid out of my coat, which was hooked on the fence, and ran until I reached the forest.*

Tomasz was one of 400 prisoners who managed to escape from Sobibór that day. Many of the escapees were killed by land mines before they reached the forest. Still others were shot by Nazi guards and German military troops, some of whom chased the escapees in airplanes. Of the prisoners who did reach freedom, only about 30 lived to the end of the war.

Rumors that the escapees carried gold made many of them victims of attack by local townspeople. Others simply could not survive in the forests during Poland's hard winters.

The revolt caused Himmler to close Sobibór just two days later. Worried that the escapees would tell other people about the mass murder, he instructed the remaining prisoners to destroy all traces of the camp—buildings, prisoner records, railway documents. Himmler wanted no evidence left of the more than 200,000 human beings who had perished there.

Italy Turns on Germany

On October 13, 1943, the day before the revolt at Sobibór, Italy declared war on Germany. This brought an end to the seven-year alliance between the two countries. Even though they had been allies, relations between Italy and Germany were very strained. Hitler and Italian leader Benito Mussolini were rivals in the fight to conquer new lands. But the German military was much stronger than the Italian, and by 1943 Italy was just a pawn controlled by Germany. Disgusted with their weak leader's inability to defy Hitler, the Italians overthrew Mussolini on July 25.

Three months later, the Italians declared war on Germany, which infuriated Hitler. He unleashed his fury on Italy's 37,000

Jews. Within just three days, approximately 1,000 Jewish residents of Rome, the Italian capital, were seized by the SS and deported to Auschwitz–Birkenau. This was only the beginning. By mid-November, more than 8,300 Italian Jews had been shipped to the camps, and some 7,700 of them were murdered there. More deportations followed. Among the deportees was Primo Levi, a chemist who many years later received international acclaim for his writing.

In many parts of Europe, Jews who were scheduled for deportation were taken first to "detention" or "transit" camps. They were held there until trains were ready to haul them to camps in Poland. Levi was sent to a huge detention camp near the Italian city of Modena. In his book *Survival in Auschwitz*, he described the scene in that camp on the night before deportation:

> *That evening the children were given no homework. . . and it was such a night that one knew that human eyes would not witness it and survive. Everyone felt this: not one of the guards, neither Italian nor German, had the courage to come and see what men do when they know they have to die.*
>
> *All took leave from life in the manner which most suited them. . . . The mothers stayed up to prepare the food for the journey with tender care, and washed their children and packed the luggage; and at dawn the barbed wire was full of children's washing hung out in the wind to dry. Nor did they forget the diapers, the toys, the cushions and the hundred other small things which mothers remember and which children always need. Would you not do the same? If you and your child were going to be killed tomorrow, would you not give him [food] to eat today?*

During deportation, more than 100 people would be loaded into a single train car, which would normally be used to carry cattle. Here they rode, crammed together without food, water, or toilets. Many of them died during their two- or three-day voyage. Cecilia Bernstein, who was a teenager when her family was deported, remembered her trip this way:

[The train] was so crowded, we took off our shoes so we wouldn't step on someone. We had no food. My brother Ari fainted from hunger. My mother cried, "Ari is dying in my hands!" But he wasn't quite dead. He would die later in Auschwitz.

Although many Nazis would later deny the role they had played in the deportation process, it is clear that Heinrich Himmler and other party officials knew exactly what was going on. In fact, they tried hard to conceal their roles by never speaking publicly about their actions. In an October 1943 speech to SS leaders on the subject of the "elimination of the Jews," Himmler cautioned:

We can talk about it quite frankly among ourselves and yet we will never speak of it publicly. . . . This is a glorious page in our history and one that has never been written and can never be written.

Life Among the Partisans

By late 1943, panic was mounting swiftly among the Jews in Europe. Some of the young, single people decided to take their chances and run rather than to await deportation and probable death. Although the number of Jews who did try to escape or resist was relatively small, their desire was great. Most of those who did escape fled to join partisan groups, to take action against the Germans. Partisans included both Jews and Gentiles. They were part of a large resistance movement that operated in most European countries during the war. Some groups were small; others numbered in the hundreds.

Partisans' lives were neither comfortable nor safe. Often they were based in remote areas, forests, or mountains. To weaken the German military effort, they blew up bridges and highways, disrupted train travel, destroyed supply depots, and staged attacks on soldiers patrolling areas where troops were encamped.

Zdenka Novak was a 24-year-old Jewish woman when she became a partisan in Yugoslavia's underground movement. Two

A portrait of the young members of a resistance group called Irgun Brit Zion (ABZ) from Kovno, Lithuania, 1943.

years earlier, in 1941, her close-knit family had been torn apart when the Germans entered her hometown of Zagreb and hauled her husband, parents, and sister away to a labor camp to await deportation.

Zdenka worked with the partisans as a secretary, translating letters, filing important papers stolen from the Germans, typing, and doing other office work. Like most partisans, her group lived constantly on the alert, always just one step ahead of discovery

Boris Yochai, a Jewish partisan from Vilnius, Lithuania, plants dynamite on a railroad track. He successfully destroyed 12 trains.

and capture. It was not unusual for them to pack their possessions on a moment's notice and move to a new location. Novak later describes one of those times:

> *Everything movable was packed in a hurry, thrown on lorries [trucks], cars, motorcycles, carts, whatever vehicles were available, and off we went. . . . The caravan then hurtled in the direction of the woods until it arrived at a place impassable by vehicles. There everything was abandoned except the things we could carry. . . . If the enemy did not reach that far, these things were gradually transported into the forest. The thorny road continued deep, deep into the forest, far away from human habitation.*

Schindler and His List

Near the Polish suburb of Plaszow, outside the city of Cracow, businessman Oskar Schindler operated a ceramics factory that manufactured kitchen utensils. Schindler's factory made good money selling its products to the German Army. Like many other factory owners, Schindler employed Jews, but, unlike most of the others, he was kind to his Jewish workers. He was also on good terms with the Gestapo and claimed many high-ranking Nazi friends.

In March 1943, when the remaining Jews in the Cracow ghetto were scheduled for deportation to a labor camp in Plaszow, Schindler brought them to his factory to keep them safe. With his own money, he provided food, medical care, and housing for these people. In September 1944, the Nazis ordered the ceramics factory closed. This meant that Schindler's workers would be deported to death camps in Poland, and he went into action to save them. He located a factory in Czechoslovakia that could be used to manufacture guns and ammunition. By October, Schindler had drawn up a list of more than 1,000 "skilled workers" needed to operate the factory. The list included Jews who had been with him at the ceramics factory, along with their friends, family members, and others he hoped to save.

Through some mistake, however, the women in the group were deported to Auschwitz–Birkenau. Using all his charm and whatever bribery he could arrange, Schindler convinced SS officials to release the women and reunite them with their families at his munitions factory. Altogether Oskar Schindler saved more than 1,500 people. His story was the subject of Steven Spielberg's Academy Award–winning movie *Schindler's List*, based on the novel by Thomas Keneally.

Oskar Schindler (left) near his factory in Poland, about 1943.

Over the years, partisan groups across Europe did substantial damage to the Germans. They helped to save people from deportation and death by providing them with the essentials of food, shelter, and supplies. They also created great confusion and disruption among German operations, as proven by the Germans' own records.

The Soviets Advance from the East

The partisans were not the only ones who were putting pressure on the Germans. By late 1943, Soviet troops were advancing from the east toward German-occupied Poland. The Nazis' reaction to the Soviet advance was to increase the number of deportations and killings. At the extermination camp of Majdanek, more than 18,000 people were murdered in a single day. "Harvest Home Festival" was what the Nazis called the massacre on November 3, 1943. Wrote historian Konnilyn Feig:

> *First, the guards herded the Jews into Field Five and ordered them to strip. Then they drove the naked Jews to the ditches and forced them to lie, face down. The SS machine-gunned them. The next group of victims had to place themselves atop the layers of corpses before they were shot. That process went on until the ditches filled.*

Throughout the winter and spring of 1943–1944, Soviet troops moved closer to Majdanek as they fought their way toward Germany. Worried that the Soviets would find evidence of the hundreds of thousands of victims who had been killed at Majdanek, the Nazis began to move all the remaining prisoners farther and farther west—away from the ever-advancing Soviet troops—to other camps in Poland and Germany. When there were not enough trains to carry them, victims were forced to march on foot.

But Majdanek was so bad that prisoners considered it a blessing to be sent to Auschwitz–Birkenau. "A transfer to Auschwitz," explained Feig, "actually raised an inmate's life expectancy."

Maintaining a Will to Live

To survive in camp, a prisoner had to maintain a will to live. Giving up hope, ceasing to care, was a certain route to death. Auschwitz–Birkenau survivor Helen Waterford recalled that maintaining daily personal habits was extremely important:

> *The "wash barrack" had only cold water and no one had soap, a towel or a rag. . . . Still, it was most important to me to water down my body (you could not call this bathing), for it helped prove to myself that I was still the same strong-willed individual, a personal victory.*

During the winter of 1944–1945, Elie Wiesel, who later won the Nobel Prize, was a 16-year-old prisoner. His father, Shlomo, was with him, and together they gave each other courage and hope. But as the selection of prisoners for death grew larger and more frequent, the elder Wiesel sensed he would be one of the next.In his book *Night*, Elie Wiesel told how Shlomo began to give up hope, and how desperately Elie tried to save him:

> *He spoke quietly. . . . "Look, take this knife," he said to me. "I don't need it any longer. It might be useful to you. And take this spoon as well. Don't sell them. Quickly! Go on. Take what I'm giving you."*
>
> *"Don't talk like that, Father." (I felt that I would break into sobs.) "I don't want you to say that. Keep the spoon and knife. You need them as much as I do. We shall see each other again this evening, after work."*
>
> *He looked at me with his tired eyes, veiled with despair. He went on: "I'm asking this of you. . . . Take them. Do as I ask, my son. We have no time. . . . Do as your father asks."*

"Butterflies Don't Live Here in the Ghetto"

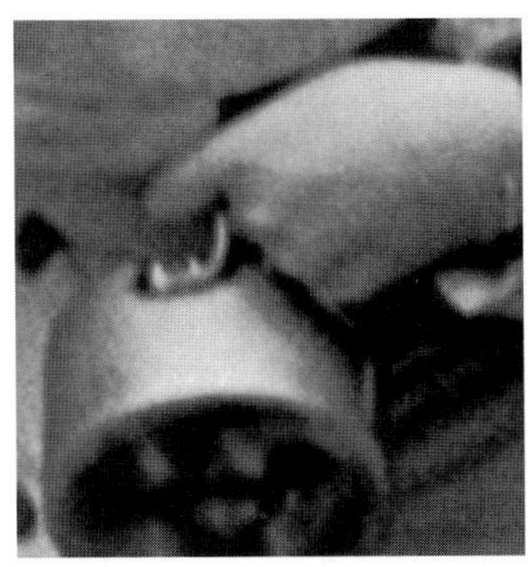

A strange odor strikes you as you walk across the glass bridge onto the second floor of the United States Holocaust Memorial Museum in Washington, D.C. It is the smell of old leather emanating from the 4,000 shoes lying in a large display bin. These are some of the 500,000 shoes collected from prisoners at the Majdanek death camp from 1942 until it was evacuated in March 1944. A *Life* magazine reporter present at the liberation wrote that the shoes brought the "full emotional shock" of the Holocaust upon him:

> *In some places the shoes had burst out of the building like corn from a crib. It was monstrous. . . . I looked at them and saw their owners: skinny kids in soft, white, worn slippers; thin ladies in black high-laced shoes; sturdy soldiers in brown military shoes.*

A teenage Dutch Jewish girl arrives at Theresienstadt in February 1944.

Hungarian Jews Marked for Death

Although the advance of the Soviet Army caused the Nazis to evacuate their easternmost death camp, it did nothing to slow the rate of deportations from the west. In fact, as the prospect of defeat loomed ever larger for the Germans, pressure on the Jews and other victims increased. Hitler was particularly upset with the Hungarian government because it had done little to dispose of its more than 700,000 Jews. Thus he announced that Germany would occupy Hungary. In March 1944, it did, and a new government controlled by the SS took charge.

That same day, Adolf Eichmann, the SS leader in charge of deportations, arrived in Hungary. He ordered Jewish community leaders to establish a *Judenrat*—a Council of Jews who would

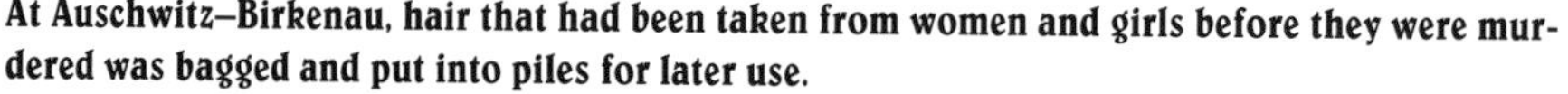

At Auschwitz–Birkenau, hair that had been taken from women and girls before they were murdered was bagged and put into piles for later use.

carry out the Germans' deportation orders. Other German-occupied countries of Europe already had such councils, in which Jews were forced to help round up others on the promise that they and their families would be spared. Like most promises the Germans made, this one was usually broken.

Within four months, more than 437,402 Hungarian Jews, including about 50,000 from the Budapest area, had been shipped to their deaths in Auschwitz–Birkenau. But Eichmann wanted more. Only a very few, sometimes just a dozen from each trainload, were kept alive. They would be used as slave laborers.

By then, word of the mass murder of Hungarian Jews had begun to spread. World leaders began putting pressure on the German-controlled Hungarian government to stop the slaughter. At last, on July 8, the government gave in to pressure and the deportations ceased—in time to save some 200,000 Jews still living in the Budapest area.

Greek Jews Become Targets

By October 1943, the once-neutral country of Greece had also been occupied by the Germans. Within days, the entire Jewish population of about 70,000 was required to register with the German occupiers. In March 1944, the Gestapo began a search for more than 10,000 Greek Jews. About half fled to the mountains or to join partisan groups. The rest were caught and deported to Auschwitz–Birkenau. The trip, with people packed into sealed cattle cars, took eight days. Hundreds died en route.

From the island of Corfu, off the western coast of Greece, around 1,800 Jews were deported to Auschwitz–Birkenau. The women were shipped mostly by land, while men traveled the first leg by sea. They had nothing to eat or drink during the voyage, which lasted 15 days. When finally they arrived at the camp, approximately 1,600 were sent immediately to the gas chambers. The other 200 were "spared" to do slave labor.

On the island of Crete, off the southern coast of Greece, some 260 Jews were rounded up by the Gestapo. They were put on a

Rachel and Joseph Chasid—Greek Jews—pose wearing their mandatory Stars of David in a ghetto in Salonika, Greece.

ship with hundreds of other prisoners and sent toward the island of Santorini, which lay across the Aegean Sea. After traveling more than 120 miles, the ship was deliberately sunk by Nazi sympathizers. All on board drowned.

The Young Die First

The Nazis had no special sympathy for Jewish children. "Nits breed lice" was an expression they used, meaning that the young would only grow up to produce more of what the Nazis considered to be "subhumans." Children were shipped to ghettos and concentration camps by the thousands. At the death camps, they were often among the first to be killed.

This peaceful image of children at rest was included in a Nazi propaganda film about Theresienstadt. Actual conditions in the camp bore no resemblance to this.

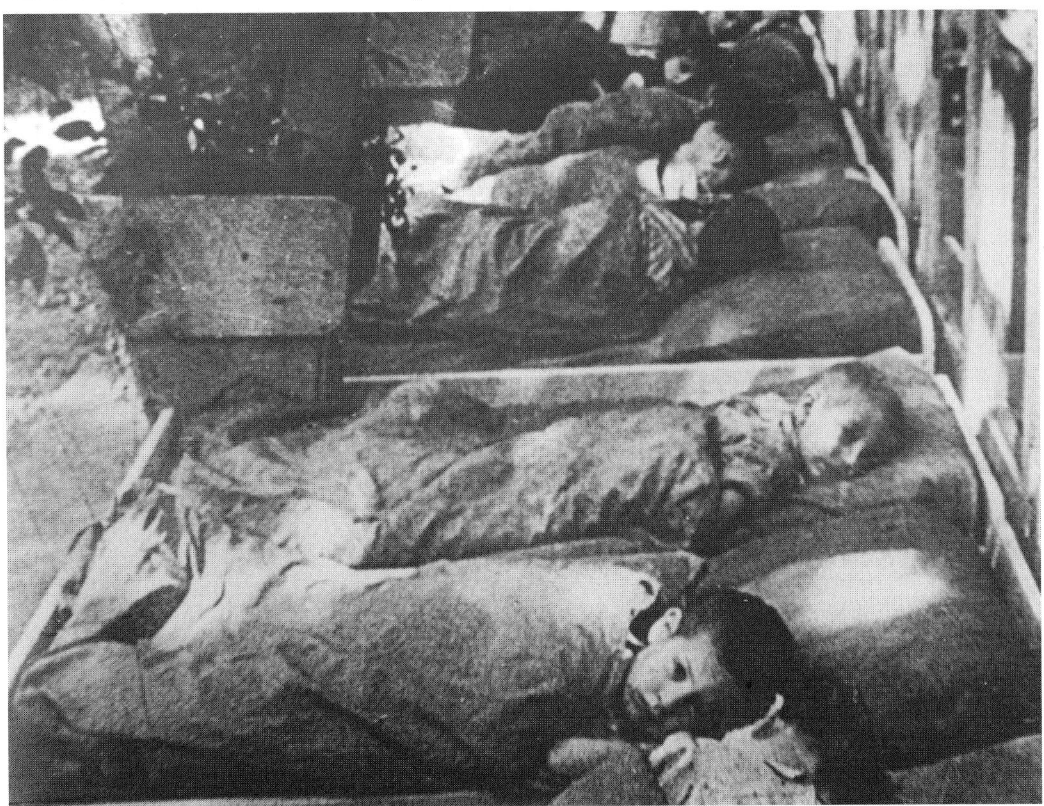

Theresienstadt was a concentration camp located in the town of Terezin, outside Prague, Czechoslovakia. It had started as a ghetto. Approximately 15,000 children under the age of 15 passed through the camp's gates from 1942 to 1945. Theresienstadt was built as a "model" by the Nazis and called "The *Führer's* [the leader's—that is, Hitler's] gift to the Jews." In an ironic way, it was actually a center of culture; many Jewish artists, intellectuals, and writers were shipped there.

One section of Theresienstadt was a "showcase" to which the Germans invited Red Cross workers and foreign leaders who wanted to "observe" the Nazis' treatment of prisoners. It was there that important prisoners were shipped—people whose disappearance might prove embarrassing to the Nazis. When a group of Swedish Red Cross officials visited the "spruced up" portion of Theresienstadt on June 23, 1944, they saw none of the filth, starvation, and disease that existed in the rest of the camp. Instead, the barracks were freshly painted, the sidewalks were clean, and flower beds decorated the grounds. This section of the camp looked like a vacation resort. There were playgrounds and parks (built by the prisoners), and an orchestra of well-fed inmates played in the "town square." So impressed were the Swedish Red Cross visitors that, when they returned home, they reported that Theresienstadt was more "an ideal suburban community than a ghetto-camp."

This propaganda was exactly what the Nazis wanted the Red Cross to believe. The Swedish workers had been successfully shielded from the thousands of tortured and starving inmates elsewhere in Theresienstadt.

Of the more than 15,000 children who passed through Theresienstadt, only about 100 lived to the end of the war. None of those survivors was under age 14. "The Jewish children in Theresienstadt were doomed," wrote historian Konnilyn Feig. But the children left behind a collection of poems, artwork, and stories that ensured their suffering would never be forgotten. One such story was written by 15-year-old Petr Fischl:

We got used to sleeping without a bed . . . to undeserved slaps, blows, and executions. We got accustomed to seeing people die in their own excrement, to seeing piled-up coffins full of corpses, to seeing the sick amid dirt and filth and to seeing the helpless doctors. We got used to it that from time to time, one thousand unhappy souls would come here and that, from time to time, another thousand unhappy souls would go away. . . .

Shortly after he wrote this piece, Fischl was shipped from Theresienstadt to Auschwitz–Birkenau, where he was killed in 1944. Petr's writing, along with the verses and artwork of dozens of other ghetto children, has been preserved in a book entitled *I Never Saw Another Butterfly*. The title comes from a line in a poem by victim Pavel Friedmann called "The Butterfly," and it illustrates how bleak life was at Theresienstadt. Friedmann's poem laments the fact that nothing as beautiful and delicate as a butterfly could survive there:

For seven weeks I've lived here,
Penned up inside this ghetto.
But I have found what I love here.
The dandelions call to me
And the white chestnut branches in the court.
Only I never saw another butterfly.

That butterfly was the last one.
Butterflies don't live here,
In the ghetto.

"We Didn't Know"

Since the devastating loss of Operation Barbarossa—the German campaign against the Soviet Union that ended in February 1943—German defeats on the battlefield had been mounting. In May 1943, Allied troops pushed German forces out of North Africa. Five months later, Italy declared war on Germany. By June 1944, Allied forces had driven the Nazis out of Rome and much of the rest of Italy. With each loss, Hitler's will to "exterminate the vermin [as he called Jews] throughout Europe" became ever stronger. He was certain that "the world of the future [would] be eternally grateful" to him for killing off the Jews.

Throughout Europe, but particularly in Germany and Poland, most Gentiles had become reluctant to help the Jews. The consequences of doing so were clear and severe—deportation and death to themselves and their families. This fear, along with continued

This photograph of a death march from Dachau was taken by a German civilian who watched as columns of prisoners filed by. Many people are known to have documented similar events.

antisemitism, convinced many people to pay no attention to the treatment of the Jews. After the war, many Germans claimed they did not realize how savagely the Jews were treated. "We didn't know, we didn't know," *Life* magazine photographer Margaret Bourke-White remembered them saying. But, she claimed, "They did know." They simply chose to look the other way.

Had everyone turned their backs on the Jews—as so many people did—Hitler might have eventually achieved his goal. Fortunately, however, there were some who were not afraid to help their neighbors. Among them were the people of Le Chambon, a tiny mountain farming village in German-occupied central France.

Le Chambon was made up primarily of Protestants. Its church was headed by a minister, Andre Trocme, and his wife Magda. Even though it was well known that a family who took a Jew into its home would be sent to a concentration camp or killed, nearly all the people of the village defied the German threat. "When their hearts spoke to them," wrote filmmaker Pierre Sauvage, who was born in Le Chambon, "they first listened, then they acted."

Why did these farmers take such a risk when so many others were unwilling? Magda Trocme explained:

> *Those of us who received the first Jews did what we thought had to be done. . . . How could we refuse them? A person doesn't sit down and say I'm going to do this and this and that. We had no time to think. . . . The issue was: Do you think we are all brothers or not?*
>
> *. . . Maybe later on in their lives, young people will be able to go through experiences of this kind—seeing people murdered, killed, or accused improperly. . . [and] they will be able to think that there always have been some people in the world who tried—who will try—to give hope, to give love, and give help to those who are in need, whatever the need is.*

The Allies Storm Ashore

After nearly four years of endangering themselves to help their fellow countrymen, the people of Le Chambon were relieved shortly after D-Day, June 6, 1944. On that date, Allied armies

Allied forces landed on the beaches of Normandy in northern France on June 6, 1944 (D-Day).

made up of American, British, and Canadian troops landed at Normandy, on the northern coast of France. On D-Day, what was known as "Fortress Europa" was finally invaded. Immediately after landing, Allied troops headed south to free the capital city of Paris from the Nazis.

These additional military setbacks only made Hitler more determined to accomplish the Final Solution. The Gestapo acted quickly to kill French Jews or anyone who was thought to be sympathetic to them. In the village of Oradour-sur-Glane, in northern France, 642 villagers were murdered. Historian Martin Gilbert wrote:

Gloucester Library
P.O. Box 2380
Gloucester, VA 23061

> *The women and children were burned alive in the church, and the men were machine-gunned, as a reprisal [revenge] against the killing in another village of an SS army commander. . . . Only seven of the villagers were Jews; the rest were killed because they had helped Jews and resisted the Nazis.*

Gloucester Library
P.O. Box
Gloucester, VA 23061

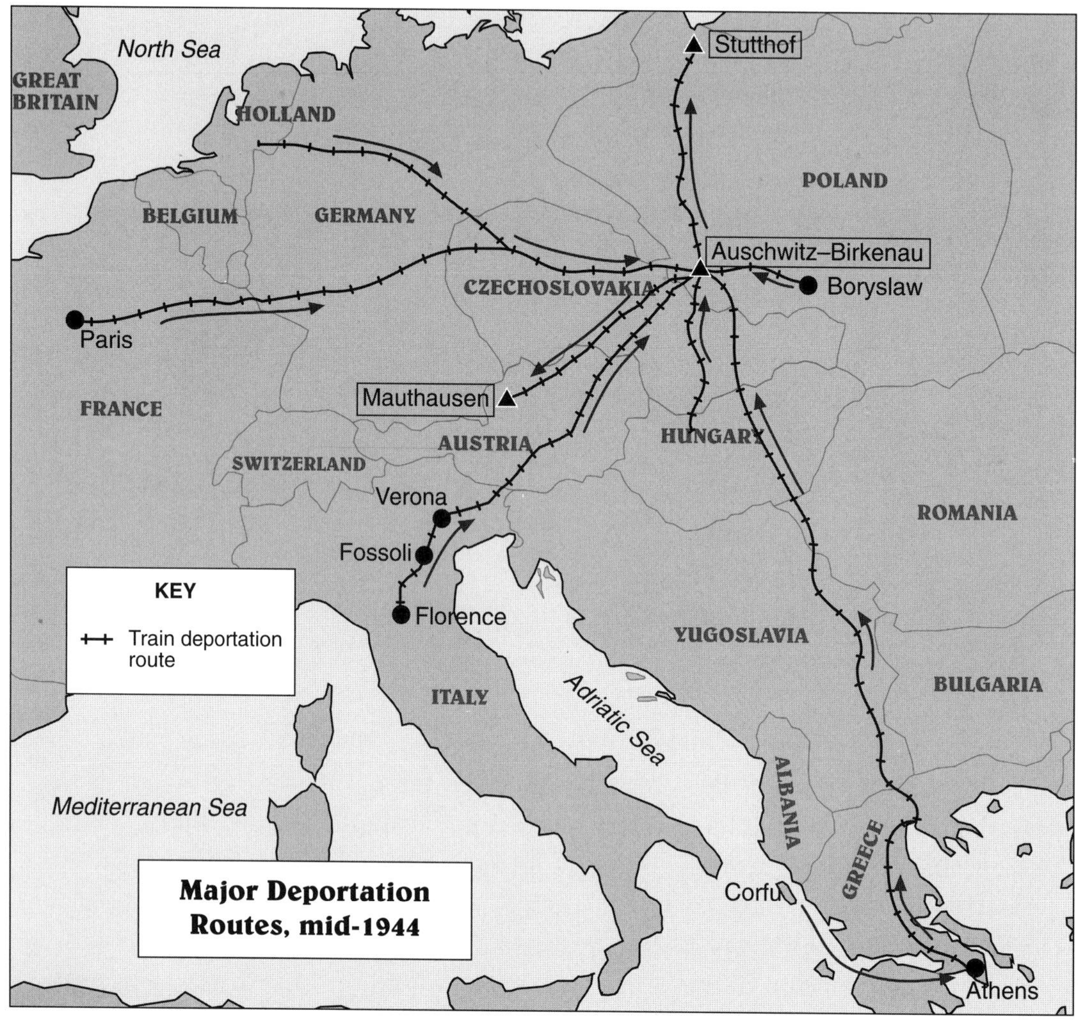

Major Deportation Routes, mid-1944

With the Allied invasion of the European continent, deportations reached a new high. On June 30, a death train left Paris for Auschwitz–Birkenau with about 1,150 people aboard. The same day, trains bound for death camps left from Italy, Holland, Poland, Greece, and Hungary. On the outside of most cars were printed the words GERMAN WORKERS-RESETTLERS.

At the same time, the Nazis moved thousands of prisoners from Polish camps westward to camps in Germany and the occupied countries that made up the Third Reich. Two of the most common destinations were Dachau and Bergen-Belsen, huge German camps that housed many political prisoners. Adding these multitudes of people to the already overcrowded camps created even greater problems of disease and starvation.

Underground Strength

As Soviet troops moved closer to Vilnius and Kovno (Lithuania) and Lublin (Poland), the Jews remaining in these ghettos decided that they had little to lose by trying to escape. They were sure to die if they stayed in the ghettos, for the Nazis would never turn them over alive to Soviet liberators. If they could escape to join partisan groups, they at least stood a chance of living to the end of the war.

The largest of these partisan groups in Europe was the Bielskis, who operated in the forests of Belorussia, just east of the Polish border and southeast of Vilnius. By 1944, the Bielski partisans numbered more than 1,200 members. Organized by Tuvia Bielski and his two brothers, the group's purpose was not only to seek revenge against the Germans but, more important, to gather and protect Jews trying to escape from the Nazis. The Bielskis' was the largest armed rescue operation of Jews by other Jews during World War II. The Bielski brothers refused to become victims of the Nazis and were determined to help any other Jew who had the same desire. "Life is difficult," Tuvia would tell newcomers. "We are in danger all the time, but if we perish, if we die, we die like human beings."

The Bielskis repaired guns, made clothes, resoled shoes, supplied services to other partisan units, and even set up a hospital and a school.

A German firing squad prepares to execute a member of the French resistance in Rochefort.

Although Tuvia Bielski lost his parents, wife, and two brothers to the Nazis, he continued to believe "that it was more important to save one Jew than to kill twenty Germans." No one—not even the sick or elderly who might have been a burden or a danger to the rest of the group—was ever turned away by the Bielskis.

In July 1944, Jews trying to escape Nazi persecution suddenly found themselves in even greater danger. For several months, some of Hitler's generals had considered him insane and had plotted to assassinate him, but those plots had failed. On July 20, however, a plot led by Colonel Count Claus Stauffenberg nearly succeeded. Stauffenberg carried a briefcase armed with a bomb to a meeting with Hitler and other top Nazis. Placing the case under a meeting table, Stauffenberg excused himself to make a phone call. When the bomb went off, four people died, but Hitler was only injured. Nevertheless, he went mad with rage, immediately taking out his anger on thousands of innocent people, including some of his own officers. There was a wave of arrests. Hitler ordered many of his top military leaders, along with more Jews, sent to concentration or death camps.

A band of Lithuanian partisans celebrates liberation in Vilnius, July 1944.

Lodz ghetto Jews are led to a deportation train bound for Auschwitz–Birkenau in the summer of 1944. The march is led by two Jewish policemen from the ghetto.

That same day, the SS ordered all Jewish orphans around Paris to be arrested—approximately 500 children. Nearly 300 of them were deported to Auschwitz–Birkenau, along with some 1,000 Jewish adults. Most were gassed on arrival, including all the children.

In August 1944, the last residents of Poland's Lodz ghetto—approximately 70,000 people—were deported to Auschwitz–Birkenau. SS head Heinrich Himmler ordered the liquidation of the Romani camp there, where, over the years, more than 20,000 Romani had lived together in family units. Now the remaining 3,000 men, women, and children were gassed. The Nazis were destroying anyone in their path whom they considered "undesirable."

A Life in Hiding

As Nazi terror and the number of deportations increased during 1944, the few Jews still living in Germany and the western portion of the Reich—those who could make the necessary arrangements—went into hiding. The underground—a communications network set up by people resisting the Nazis—helped to keep those in hiding supplied with food, places to live, and information from the outside world. But living in hiding was difficult and dangerous, and all too often the Gestapo was successful in finding the fugitives.

Helen and Siegfried Wohlfarth lived in hiding on the third floor of a house near Amsterdam, Holland, in the summer of 1944. Earlier, they had given up their five-year-old daughter, Doris, to total strangers because living in hiding was especially difficult for children. As they said later, they wanted Doris "to have every chance to stay alive, even if it were not possible for us." On August 25, 1944—the same day Allied soldiers liberated the city of Paris—four Gestapo officers in plain clothes discovered the home where Helen and Siegfried were hiding. Later, Helen wrote about the day she had dreaded—the day that she and her husband were discovered:

> *They looked through our few belongings, and suggested that we take some warm clothing because where we were going the weather would be cold. . . . Searching further, they found a picture of Doris. . . . "If this is your child, or if you have more children in hiding, we advise you to take them along," they suggested. "You will be going to live in a family camp, and while you are working, the children will be cared for."*

It was all a lie, and the Wohlfarths knew it. They took no warm clothing, for they knew where they were headed and were already hoping for a chance to escape. They stayed silent about Doris; they also knew that there was no "family camp" awaiting them. Helen later learned that "head-money" was being offered for every Jew the Gestapo rounded up. The Gestapo agents would have received additional money if they had brought in Doris as well.

The Wohlfarths were taken from their hiding place to a prison in Amsterdam, where the prisoners were separated into two groups, men and women. Helen wrote:

> *If [the other people] knew about the extermination camps, if the name Auschwitz meant anything to them, they did not say. No one talked about the future or speculated on the plans of the Nazis. Many women prayed quietly or talked softly with each other.*

Major Death Marches, Deportations, and Uprisings, August 1944

After two days, Helen and Siegfried were moved to the Westerbork transit camp to await deportation. With the Nazis' stepped-up campaign of terror and increased number of deportations, trains now ran east from Westerbork, usually to Auschwitz–Birkenau, every Tuesday, with at least 1,000 Jews on each train. At Westerbork, anxious prisoners begged frantically for news of loved ones or for information about where they were headed. "Rumors about the destination were everywhere," Helen Wohlfarth recalled. "Nobody knew the full truth and nobody would have believed the reality."

"We Had Been Counted"

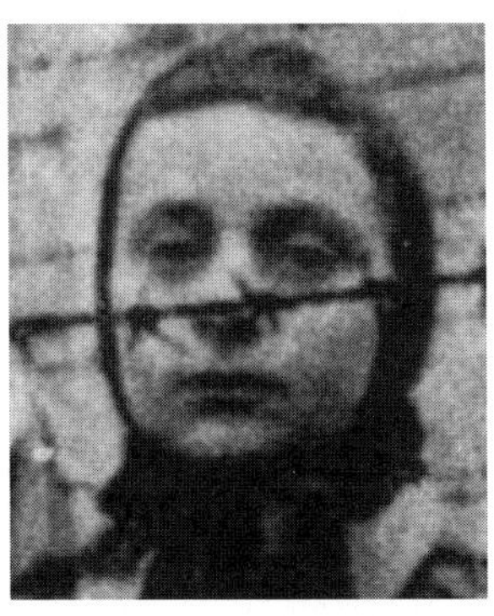

Two trains left Holland for Auschwitz–Birkenau on September 3 and 4, 1944, carrying more than 3,100 people. Helen and Siegfried Wohlfarth were on the first train, along with Anne Frank and her family. Anne's diary would later become the most famous first-person account of the Holocaust. The trip to the camps lasted three days. Many of the people died during the journey.

Upon arrival, men and women were separated into two columns, and Helen found herself beside a woman and a little girl. Of that moment, Helen wrote:

> *They, too, had been arrested in hiding and were told. . . to take children out of hiding because we would be located in family camps where they would receive care. For a very short time I had a gnawing feeling that we had made the wrong decision in leaving our child with strangers. But this soon changed. . . .*

Children stand between two rows of barbed wire at Auschwitz–Birkenau.

[On the platform was] a remarkably good-looking officer in a well-tailored uniform and highly polished boots. . . . The officer looked us over and asked if this were my child, which I naturally denied. With no other word he pointed his right thumb in the direction the woman and her child should go and his left one for me to follow.

The woman and her daughter were probably dead within hours, for children were sent immediately to the gas chambers with their mothers. Much later, Helen realized that the good-looking officer was Dr. Josef Mengele. Nicknamed the "Angel of Death," Mengele was the notorious chief medical officer at Auschwitz–Birkenau. This position put him in charge of all the

A U.S. soldier stands guard over a group of captured German prisoners, somewhere on the western front, 1944.

"selections" of prisoners for the gas chamber. Sometimes he used his thumb, sometimes he pointed with his riding crop, but every prisoner in the selection had to go left or right—one way to life, the other way to death.

Revolt of the "Special Detail"

As the Nazis stepped up the pace of the Final Solution, they forced more prisoners to work in the killing centers to make the process go faster. Twenty-two-year-old Filip Müller was on such a work crew, known as a *Sonderkommando*, or "special detail." When he arrived at Auschwitz–Birkenau, his first order was to "stir the bodies." He was taken into the crematorium, the building where the ovens were located, handed a poker, and told to poke the fire. His first reaction was to refuse such an order, but when another Jewish prisoner warned him in a whisper to do it or he would be killed, Müller obeyed.

It was important to the Nazis that members of the *Sonderkommando* never warn other prisoners of their fates. They did not want to create panic among those doomed to die. One day, however, a man working with Müller spotted his friend's wife entering the gas chamber. Recalled Müller:

> *He came right out and told her: "You are going to be exterminated. In three hours you'll be ashes." She ran all over and warned the other women. . . . When she saw that no one would listen, she scratched her whole face. Out of despair. In shock. And she started to scream.*
>
> *So what happened? Everyone was gassed. The woman was held back. We had to line up in front of the ovens. First, they tortured her horribly because she wouldn't betray him. In the end she pointed to him. He was taken out of line and thrown alive into the oven. We were told: "Whoever tells anything will end like that."*

At last, in desperation, prisoners forced to work on the *Sonderkommando* at Auschwitz–Birkenau revolted. They knew

Hitler, accompanied by other German officials, inspects damage done by Allied bombing in 1944.

that, because of all their eyes had seen, they were doomed to be killed by the Nazis, so what did they have to lose? The revolt was part of an even larger plan for a general prisoner uprising within the camp.

On October 7, 1944, when workers on the *Sonderkommando* learned that they themselves were about die, they went into action. Using homemade bombs and weapons, they blew up Crematorium Three and killed or wounded many of the SS guards. One SS guard was thrown alive into the oven.

The Ovens Go Cold

The October 7 revolt did not free many prisoners or liberate the camp, but it did make an important change in the Nazis' plans. When they saw that one small group of determined prisoners could overpower a large unit of SS guards, they abandoned their plan to kill all prisoners. Instead, they began moving them to other camps deeper within the Reich.

One group was marched northwest to Leiberose, where they were ordered to help build a retirement community for German military officers. When their work there was done, they were ordered on a 100-mile (160-kilometer) death march to the Sachsenhausen camp. Of the more than 3,500 prisoners who set out in the slush, snow, and freezing temperatures, fewer than 900 arrived alive. Those who were in the hospital at the time the march began were shot, and the building was set afire.

Other groups were moved by train. Auschwitz prisoner Helen Wohlfarth was sent to Kratzau, a women's labor camp in northern Czechoslovakia. Anne Frank and her family were also selected for deportation, Helen recalled, but Anne's mother was reluctant to leave:

> *Three hundred women were counted and brought into another barrack. The fact that we had been counted, we decided, was a very good sign. Those destined for the gas chamber were never counted. . . . Mrs. Frank and her daughter, Anne, were among the three hundred women selected. Margot, the older sister, was in quarantine for a skin eruption and Mrs. Frank did not want to leave Auschwitz without her. That night, she and Anne hid in another barrack, and the daughters, at least, were later deported to Bergen-Belsen, where they died from typhoid and malnutrition. Some reports claim that Mrs. Frank died in Auschwitz before the deportation.*

This Belgian woman, who collaborated with the Nazis during occupation, was marked with a swastika after her hair was shaved. Public shaming of collaborators was part of the post-liberation process in some countries.

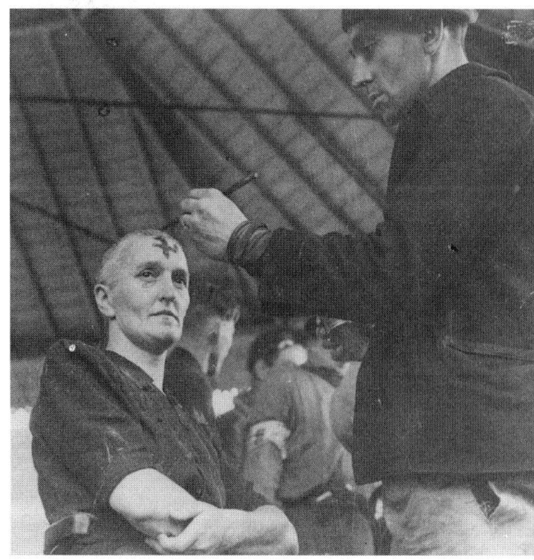

Soviet soldiers inspect a German warehouse filled with thousands of shoes taken from prisoners before their death. This warehouse contained materials from Majdanek, which had been liberated during the summer of 1944.

On November 7, one month after the *Sonderkommando* revolt at Auschwitz–Birkenau, Heinrich Himmler ordered the gassings to cease. Soviet troops were getting very close to the camp, and the Nazis knew they must hide evidence of the deaths and mass murders. On November 28, 1944, the ovens that had turned so many human bodies to ash were cold at last.

The Soviets Arrive

By New Year's Day 1945, Soviet soldiers had pushed westward nearly to Warsaw, Poland. Again the Nazis worried that liberating armies would discover the full extent of the horror of the camps, and they took steps to destroy the evidence.

The Courage of Raoul Wallenberg

Cruelty against the Jews raged across Europe in an increasing fever as Soviet troops neared Hungary in 1944. On November 2, the defiant SS rounded up nearly 50,000 of the Jews still living in Budapest and sent them on a forced march westward, toward Vienna, Austria. Perhaps as many as 10,000 died. Many more would surely have died had it not been for the intervention of Raoul Wallenberg, a diplomat from neutral Sweden.

Armed with a great deal of money and a self-assured, commanding manner, Wallenberg—at tremendous risk to himself and his family—began issuing passports and other impressive papers with the Swedish seal to keep the Jews of Budapest safe from the Nazis. "Anything that looked like an official paper, document, or list of names was flourished by. . . Wallenberg with an air of authority that intimidated even Nazi officials," wrote historian Michael Berenbaum. In the end, Wallenberg directly saved about 4,000 Jews. But nearly all of the 100,000 or so Jews who were still alive in Hungary when the Soviets arrived on January 16, 1945, owe their lives to him.

The day after the Soviets' arrival, one of Wallenberg's friends found him with a group of Soviet soldiers, working out a plan to help the Jews adapt to life after the war. No one knows what went on at that meeting or how the Soviets felt toward Raoul Wallenberg. But on January 17, Wallenberg made a strange comment to one of his closest associates: "I do not know whether I am a guest of the Soviets or their prisoner," Wallenberg told him. Shortly thereafter, the man who had saved so many lives disappeared himself. Much later, the Soviet Union announced that Wallenberg had been its prisoner and had died of a heart attack in 1947. Despite this statement, the entire truth has never been fully known.

At Chelmno, where approximately 10,000 people had been killed in 1944, the SS ordered prisoners to tear down many of the buildings and to dig up and burn the bodies that had been buried in the mass graves. On January 17, when the job was done, the *Sonderkommando* was ordered to kill the remaining Jewish workers, to complete the liquidation of the camp. The Jews revolted, killing two of the guards. In response, the SS herded the remaining Jews into a building, set it afire, and shot those who tried to escape. Only two survived.

The same day in January, Soviet troops reached the area of Auschwitz–Birkenau. In a panic to keep the tens of thousands of remaining prisoners out of Soviet hands, the SS ordered an evacuation. Prisoners were separated into three groups: those who could march, those who could walk only to the train station, and those who were too ill to walk anywhere. Perhaps as many as 66,000 prisoners were sent on forced marches to slave-labor camps in western Poland and Germany. For hundreds of miles they marched in sub-zero temperatures, some without shoes, and all without warm clothing. One of the youngest marchers, 11-year-old Thomas Buergenthal, a Czechoslovakian Jew, later explained what happened to him and two friends:

> *The children's camp group was put in front when we first marched out. . . . After about a 10 to 12 hour walk we began to be very tired. The children began to fall back. People from the back were pushing, that we weren't going fast enough. And whoever sat down was shot by guards at each side of the road.*
>
> *. . . [T]hree of us developed a system of resting, which was to run up to the front, and then sort of stop almost, until we reached the back. And by that time, we had rested, and then we could run up again and we would stay warm. Suddenly in the evening they stopped the column and asked for all the children to come forward, that they were going to put us on a farm. And we wouldn't have to march anymore. Well, [the three of us] had had experience. And we didn't go. All the children from that group were then taken away, and apparently shot. . . .*

The Machinery of Death

At the United States Holocaust Memorial Museum in Washington, D.C., is a scale model of Crematorium II, one of four killing centers at Auschwitz–Birkenau. The sculpture, created by Mieczyslaw Stobierski, shows the steps in the killing process. First, victims walked downstairs into an underground room that held about 1,000 people. There, they were told to undress and prepare to take showers.

Guards then marched the naked people underground into a large room with shower heads in the ceiling. With everyone inside, the guards sealed and locked the doors and poured pellets of Zyklon B through vents in the roof. When the pellets hit the floor, they released a poisonous gas, killing everyone in the room within minutes. It took another 20 minutes for fans to blow the bad air out of the room so the bodies could be removed.

Corpses were taken into the next room, where gold fillings were removed from the teeth and hair was shaved from the women's heads to be used by the Nazis in manufacturing various products. An elevator then lifted the bodies to the crematorium on the ground floor, where they were shoved, three or four at a time, into one of 15 ovens. In Crematorium II alone, 1,000 bodies could be burned each day.

Thomas and his friends were the only children known to have survived the three-day march.

Back in Auschwitz–Birkenau, the hundreds of prisoners who had been too weak to march were shot by the SS. At last, on the afternoon of January 27, the Soviets broke through to liberate the camp. They were horrified by what they saw. Before them lay the bodies of 648 Jews, Poles, and Romani. More than 7,000 prisoners clung thinly to life, some 150 of them children. Many more prisoners would die in the coming weeks—by then they were simply too weak to survive, even with food and medical care. But Auschwitz–Birkenau, a place that many survivors would remember as a "hell on earth," was free at last. In the three years that the camp had operated as a death center, more than 1 million people were murdered there.

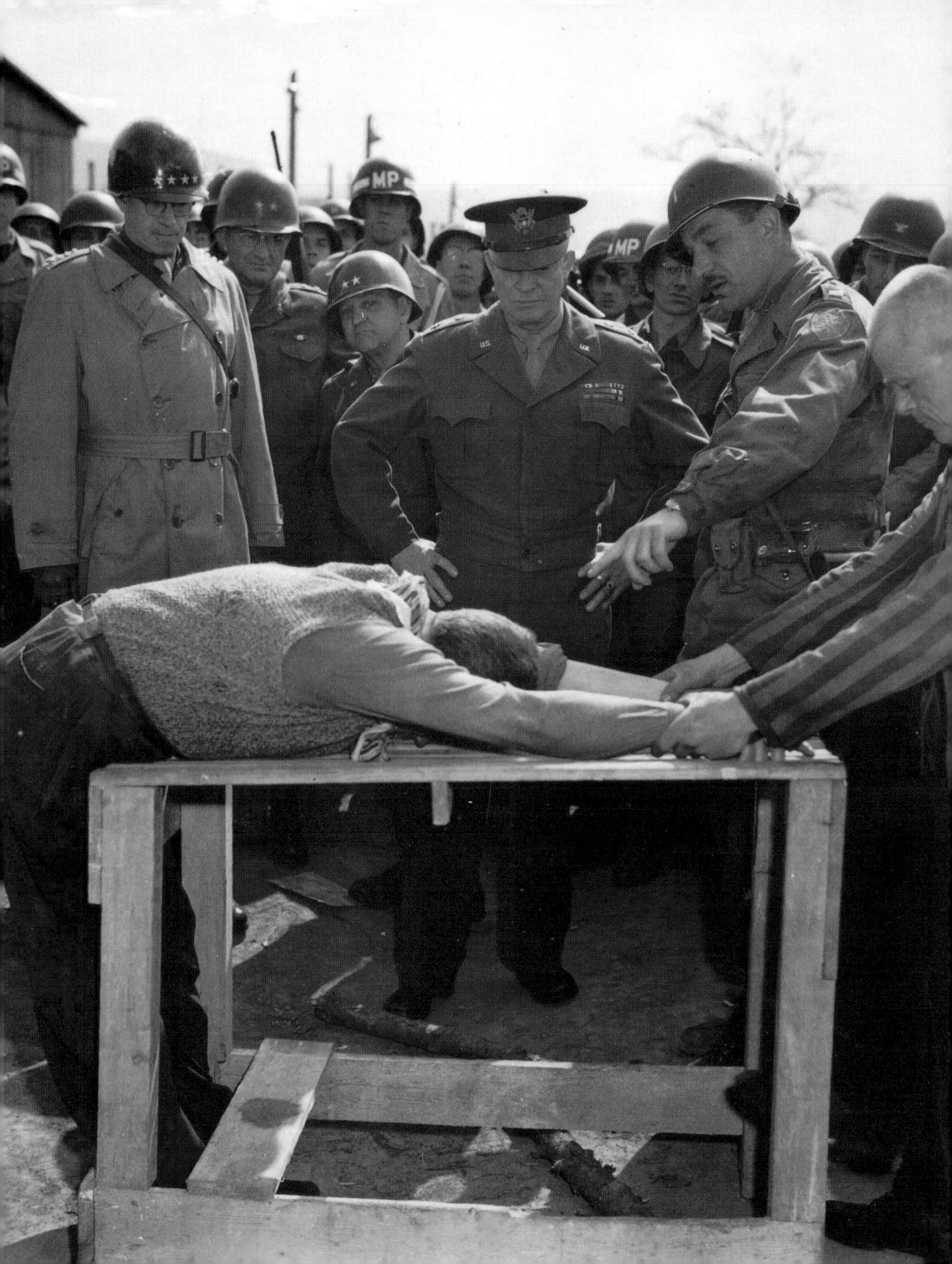
MP
MP

"Nothing but Bread"

By April 1945, it was clear, even to Adolf Hitler's closest associates, that Nazi rule would soon be over. In March, the Allies had penetrated the heartland of Germany and were now heading toward the capital city of Berlin. On April 4, American troops reached the Ohrdruf concentration camp, in east-central Germany. This was the first time that Americans had actually seen the camps. Upon his arrival, even General Dwight D. Eisenhower, a seasoned soldier and the leader of all Allied forces in Europe, was shocked. He sent pictures of the dead and dying to British prime minister Winston Churchill and encouraged world leaders to come and see for themselves.

General Eisenhower watches as former camp inmates at Gotha demonstrate how they were tortured by Nazis, 1945.

The Liberation of Buchenwald

One week later, General George Patton's American forces liberated Buchenwald, a concentration camp not far from Ohrdruf. American radio broadcaster Edward R. Murrow attempted to give his listeners an idea of the horror that awaited the soldiers. He told of piles of emaciated bodies. "[But] for most of it," he admitted, "I have no words. If I have offended you by this rather mild account of Buchenwald, I am not in the least sorry."

Among the prisoners was Elie Wiesel, who, with his father, had been moved there in the rush to evacuate Auschwitz–Birkenau. On April 10, 1945, the teenager was one of approximately 21,900 people still in camp, including several hundred children. He later wrote:

A Russian survivor liberated from Buchenwald—by U.S. troops—identifies a former camp guard who brutally beat prisoners.

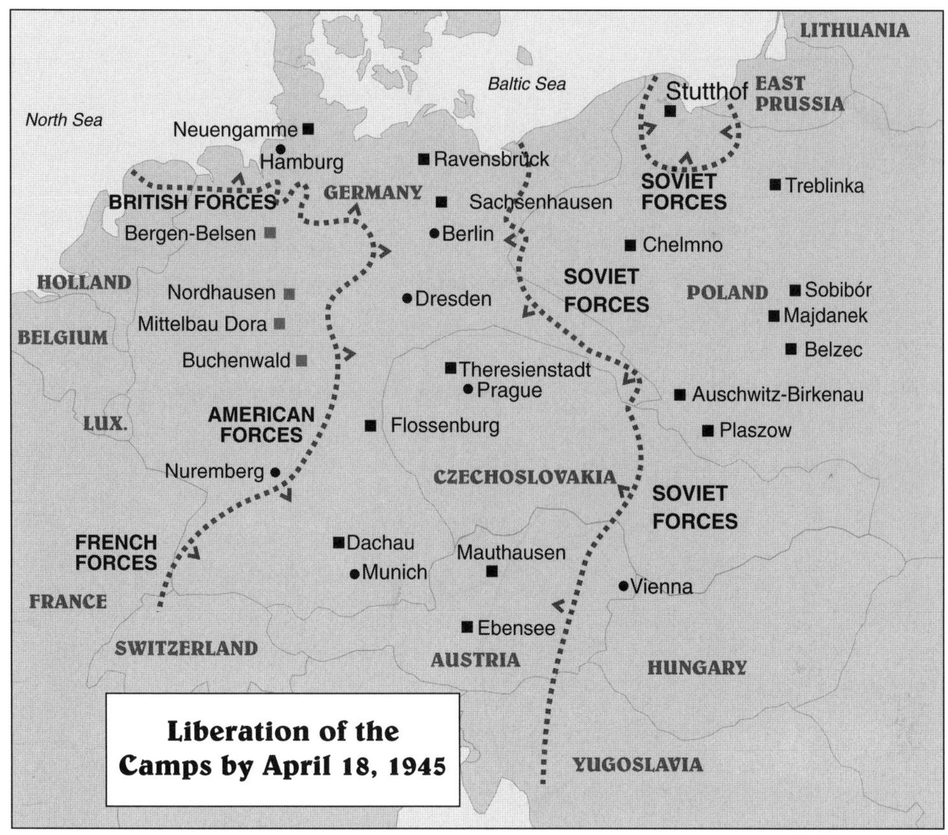

Liberation of the Camps by April 18, 1945

> *We were tormented with hunger. We had eaten nothing for six days, except a bit of grass or some potato peelings found near the kitchens. . . . [The next day] at about six o'clock in the evening, the first American tank stood at the gates of Buchenwald.*
>
> *Our first act as free men was to throw ourselves onto the provisions. We thought only of that. Not of revenge, not of our families. Nothing but bread.*

Three days later, Wiesel became ill with food poisoning and was sent to a hospital. There, he had a chance to view himself in a mirror for the first time in a year—a year of unbelievable suffering. "From the depths of the mirror," he wrote, "a corpse gazed back at me. The look in his eyes, as they stared into mine, has never left me."

"The Dead Were More Fortunate"

When Dwight D. Eisenhower's troops began liberating the concentration camps, the American general was so shocked by what he saw that he asked a group of senators and representatives to come to Germany and witness the scenes for themselves. Among them was Missouri congressman Dewey Short. The congressman visited Buchenwald, Nordhausen, and Dachau, and described the scenes this way:

> *The cruel and universal weapon was...starvation. Thousands upon thousands of miserable men have I looked at with hollowed eyes, fevered cheeks, emaciated bodies with skin dried to the bone and all hope died out of their eyes. Most of them were dead. The living dead were more awful. They could still open their eyes, but they did not see. They had ears but could scarcely hear. Their wrecked bodies and tortured minds had reduced them to a level below animals. They were helpless skeletons; hollow frames with departed souls. The dead were more fortunate than these live corpses....*
>
> *All this made me sick. I was nauseated by the foul odors in these dirty shabby barracks, by the squalor and filth of the bunks in which these overworked and underfed prisoners slept.... Six men occupied a single berth of about 5 by 3 feet [1.5 by 1 meter].... Many slept on bare boards. The best had only tattered rags to sleep on. Their bodies were covered with lice which served as a blanket. Tuberculosis was rampant. Typhus was widespread. Nearly all were suffering from dysentery....*
>
> *The unsanitary conditions were indescribably shocking. There were only a few crude toilets. Many victims were too ill and too weak to walk to them. A pig pen would have been preferred to these cesspools of hell. Again my soul cried out, "Oh, God, how can humanity sink to such depths?"*

Life magazine photographer Margaret Bourke-White was with General Patton's troops. She described her shock at what she saw:

> *Buchenwald was more than the mind could grasp. I saw and photographed the piles of naked, lifeless bodies, the human skeletons in furnaces, the living skeletons who would die the next day because they had had to wait too long for deliverance, the pieces of tattooed skin for lampshades. Using the camera was almost a relief. It [put] a slight barrier between myself and the horror in front of me.*

German citizens from a town near Namering view the bodies of more than 800 Jewish slave workers who were murdered by SS guards.

It was true. The Nazis sometimes used human body parts to make items useful to the Reich. Certain camp officers had been told that "combed-out and cut-off women's hair will be used to make socks for submarine crews, and to manufacture felt stockings for railroad workers."

Enraged by what he saw, Patton ordered his men to go into town and bring back 1,000 German civilians to witness the Nazi atrocities at Buchenwald. So outraged were the Allied soldiers that they brought back 2,000 people and made them walk through the streets of the camp.

How much did the German people know about the horror that was going on inside the camps so near their homes? And if they did know, why didn't they do something to stop it? These questions will remain forever unanswered.

Survivors in Allach, a sub-camp of Dachau, welcome liberation from arriving American troops, April 30, 1945.

Epidemic

Typhus, a disease that causes high fever, severe headache, acute diarrhea, and extreme mental confusion, killed people by the thousands at the filthy Bergen-Belsen concentration camp near Hannover, Germany. The disease, spread by body lice, was carried by nearly every prisoner. At Bergen-Belsen, in the last months of the war, typhus reached the epidemic stage.

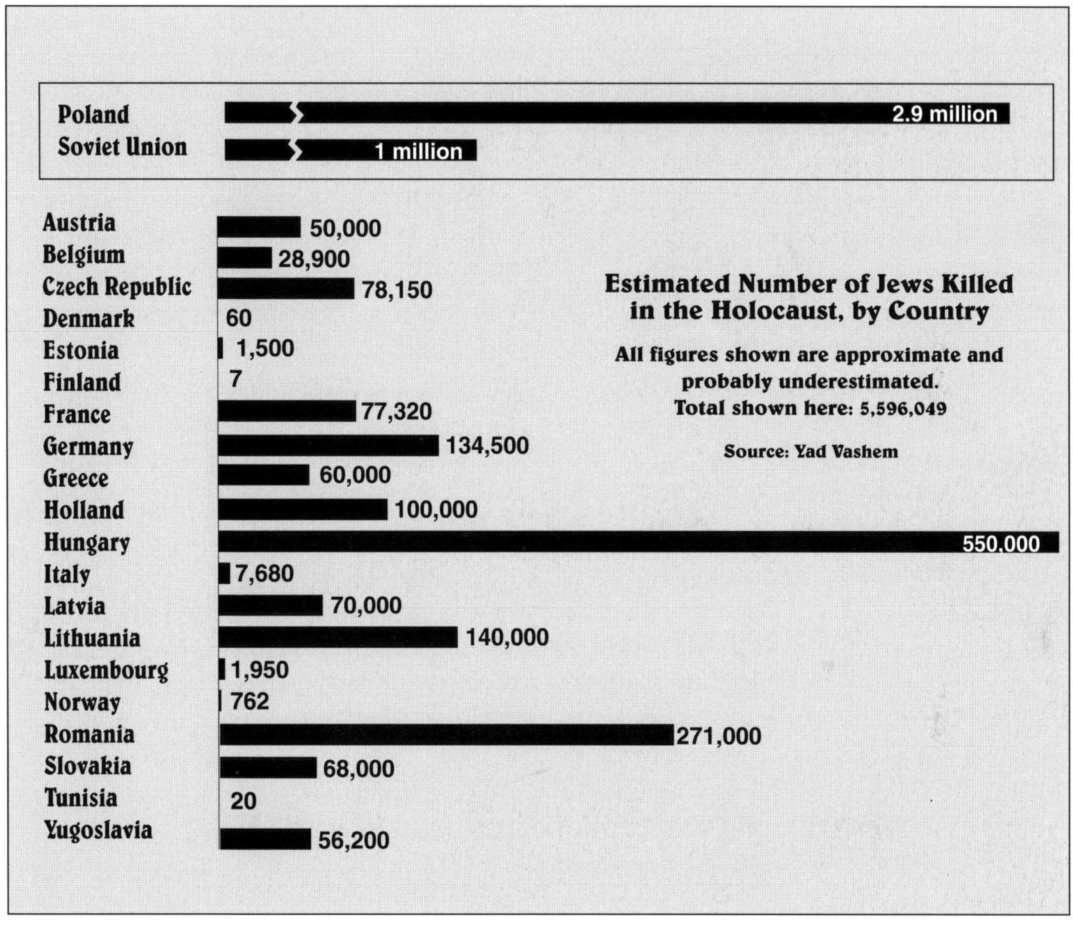

Yet, for all the deaths that typhus caused, starvation brought more. When the British soldiers arrived to liberate Bergen-Belsen on April 15, 1945, the sight of nearly 10,000 unburied bodies met their eyes. Wrote one officer:

> *We saw enormous covered death pits. One pile was uncovered. It contained. . . blackened and naked bodies. . . . In the women's compound, in full view of the children's compound. . . we saw an enormous pile of naked dead women. . . .*

Children of the Holocaust

Beneath the Children's Garden at Yad Vashem, the Israeli memorial to Holocaust survivors, is a structure built to remember the approximately 1½ million Jewish children who were murdered by the Nazis. Visitors enter a room in which a few photographs of children are hung. Then they walk down a ramp into a dark, quiet hall that is hung with panels of mirrors. The glass reflects only a few candles. The candles' flames are multiplied by the mirrors into 1½ million lights. The only sound is that of a voice reading the names, ages, and countries of the children who were killed.

But the horror that children experienced in the Holocaust was not limited to those who were killed. Children who survived found their lives in tatters from starvation, illness, fear, and loss of family and friends. Today, more than half a century after the Holocaust, many of those "child survivors" have joined groups where they can share their experiences and try to help one another heal.

One of these groups is the Hidden Child Foundation, made up of people who survived the war because they were hidden or sent to safety by their parents. Members stay in touch through a newsletter. In each issue is a listing of people who are still seeking news of family members or friends lost in the Holocaust. "Does anyone know about my sister?" asked a woman in North Carolina. "I am searching for my sister's children," wrote a woman in New York. The newsletter often prints articles by child survivors like this one by Pola Jasphy, who lived in Poland and went into hiding at age 14:

So sick were many of the living that medicine or food could not save them: More than 28,000 people who had survived the war in Bergen-Belsen died after liberation.

On April 29, 1945, a group of young American soldiers liberated Dachau, in southern Germany near Munich. So horrified were they by what they saw that many could not speak of it until they were old men. In that place—the very first Nazi concentration camp—more than 40,000 people had been murdered in the last year. "Some of the photographs taken after the liberation of Dachau are so terrible that they have never been reproduced,"

Between 1941 and 1944. . . I lost everyone I loved. My mother disappeared one day after bringing food to some cousins. . . . Soon after, my father took my brother, my aunt and me into hiding. . . . We had to move to [a farmer's] pig sty after snakes entered the storehouse [where we lived].

Jasphy explained what happened when the German Army discovered them:

They shot my father and brother, and were about to walk into [our] sty when another soldier called them away. The farmer told me and my aunt we had to leave that evening. My aunt was killed a few months later.

Jasphy, who thus became an orphan, lives today in New Jersey. Many times in her life, she has asked herself, "Why did I survive?" Such guilt is a common burden of Holocaust survivors.

wrote Martin Gilbert. The historian could not bring himself to reproduce them in his own books.

Lyle Williams, a 19-year-old American soldier with the liberation forces, described his reaction to the scene he faced at Dachau: "Unbelief, nausea, repulsion, compassion [for the victims]. Extreme anger at the captors, no mercy for the guards."

In the meantime, Soviet troops were moving toward Ravensbrück, a women's camp north of Berlin. During the previous two years, more than 92,000 victims—most of them women and children, both Jews and non-Jews—had been murdered there. As the Soviets drew nearer, the Nazis rounded up some 17,000 of those remaining in Ravensbrück and sent them west on a forced march. A Red Cross worker who was in the area later remembered what she witnessed:

> *As I approached them, I could see that they had sunken cheeks, distended bellies and swollen ankles. Their complexion was sallow. All of a sudden, a whole column of those starving wretches appeared. In each row a sick woman was supported or dragged along by her [companions]. A young SS woman supervisor with a police dog on a leash led the column, followed by two girls who incessantly hurled abuse at the poor women.*

Hitler Retreats

The final marches were pointless; Germany's defeat was less than a month away. In Berlin, Adolf Hitler retreated to his bunker, an underground complex of living quarters and office space. There, on April 29, 1945, he married his longtime mistress, Eva Braun. He had waited because, as he said, "during the years of struggle" he had not felt he "could accept the responsibility" of marriage.

But the marriage was short-lived. The next day after lunch, Hitler and Braun went to their rooms. At about 3:30 P.M., others present in the bunker heard a single shot fired. When an SS member entered the suite, he found Hitler's blood-soaked body on the sofa, a bullet through his head. Beside him lay Braun's body; she had swallowed a capsule of poison.

Liberation's Challenge

Just over a week later, on May 8, World War II in Europe ended with Germany's unconditional surrender to the Allies. Many millions lay dead; many more were displaced. For the Jews and other victims of the Holocaust, the fall of Nazi Germany was a somber victory that had come far too late.

CHRONOLOGY OF THE HOLOCAUST: 1933–1945

1933

January 30
Adolf Hitler becomes chancellor of Germany

February 28
Nazis declare emergency after Reichstag fire; consolidate power

March 22
Nazis open first concentration camp: Dachau

May 10
Public book burnings target works by Jews and opponents of the Nazis

July 14
Nazi Party established as one and only legal party in Germany

1934

January 26
German–Polish non-aggression pact signed

1935

September 15
Nuremberg Laws passed

1936

March
Germany occupies Rhineland, flouting the Versailles Treaty

August
Olympic Games held in Berlin

1937

September 7
Hitler declares end of the Versailles Treaty

1938

March 13
Anschluss: annexation of Austria

July 6–13
Evian Conference: refugee policies

September 29
Munich Conference: appeasement; Allies grant Germany Sudetenland (part of Czechoslovakia)

November 9–10
Kristallnacht: long-planned pogrom explodes across "Greater Germany"

1939

May
British White Paper: Jewish emigration to Palestine limited

August 23
Soviet–German non-aggression pact signed

September 1
Germany invades Poland; Poland falls within a month

September 2
Great Britain and France declare war on Germany

September 17
Red (Soviet) Army invades eastern Poland

October 8
First ghetto established in Poland

1940

February 12
Deportation of Jews from Germany to occupied Poland begins

Spring
Germany conquers Denmark, Norway, Belgium, Luxembourg, Holland, and France (occupies northern part)

April 27
Heinrich Himmler orders creation of Auschwitz concentration camp; established May 20

October 16
Order for creation of Warsaw ghetto

1941

March 24
Germany invades North Africa

June 22
Operation Barbarossa: invasion of the Soviet Union; German war on two fronts

July 31
Reinhard Heydrich appointed to implement "Final Solution": extermination of European Jewry

December 7
Japan attacks Pearl Harbor

December 11
Germany and Italy declare war on the United States

1942

January 20
Wannsee Conference: coordination of "Final Solution"

Spring–Summer
Liquidation of Polish ghettos; deportation of Jews to extermination camps

November 19–20
Soviet Army counterattacks at Stalingrad

1943

January 18–21
Major act of resistance in Warsaw ghetto

April 19
Bermuda Conference: fruitless discussion of rescue of Jewish victims of Nazis; liquidation of Warsaw ghetto begins

April 19–May 16
Warsaw ghetto uprising

June 11
Heinrich Himmler orders liquidation of all ghettos in Poland and the Soviet Union

October 2
Danes rescue more than 7,200 Jews from Nazis

1944

May–July
Deportation of Hungarian Jews: 437,402 sent to Auschwitz

June 6
D-Day: Allies invade Normandy

July
Soviet troops liberate Majdanek camp in Poland

1945

January 27
Soviet troops liberate Auschwitz–Birkenau

April–May
Allies liberate Buchenwald, Bergen-Belsen, Dachau, Mauthausen, and Theresienstadt concentration camps

April 30
Hitler commits suicide

May 7
Germany surrenders unconditionally to Allies

November
Nuremberg Trials begin

Glossary

Aktion A German word meaning "action" or "plan of action." The term was often used by the SS or Gestapo to mean the planned, mass roundup, deportation, or murder of Jews.

Anschluss The German annexation of Austria on March 12–13, 1938.

Anti-Semite A person who hates Jews.

Antisemitism Hatred of Jews.

Aryanization A term used by the Nazis to mean the transfer of all assets and control of German-owned businesses to Germans who were considered Aryans.

Aryans Originally, a term referring to ancient Indo–Europeans or any Indo-European language. The Nazis used the term to mean people of Northern European background, or members of what the Nazis termed the German "master race."

Concentration Camps Labor camps set up by the Nazis to house political prisoners or people they considered to be "undesirable." Prisoners were made to work like slaves and many died as a result of starvation, disease, or beatings. *Also called work camps and prison camps.*

Crematorium A building in the camps that contained the ovens, where the bodies of victims were burned. The term is sometimes used to refer to the ovens themselves.

Death's Head Brigade A division of the SS that was in charge of guarding the concentration camps. Its members were known to be extremely brutal and inhumane. Called *Totenkopf* in German.

Deportation The shipment of victims to death or concentration camps, usually by train, in cramped and unheated cattle cars.

Extermination Camps Death camps built by the Nazis in German-occupied Poland for the sole purpose of killing people. The most common method of murder used at these camps was poisonous gas. The victims' bodies were usually burned in ovens called crematoria. The six extermination camps were Auschwitz-Birkenau, Belzec, Chelmno, Majdanek, Sobibór, and Treblinka. *Also called killing centers.*

Final Solution The Nazis' term for their plan to exterminate all the Jews of Europe. The term was first used at the Wannsee Conference near Berlin on January 20, 1942.

Führer A German word meaning "leader." It was used to refer to Adolf Hitler, dictator of Germany from 1933 to 1945 and head of the Nazi Party.

Genocide The deliberate and systematic murder of an entire race, class, or large group of people.

Gentile A non-Jewish person.

Gestapo The Nazi secret police who were responsible for rounding up, arresting, and deporting victims to ghettos or camps. The Gestapo were part of the SS.

Ghetto In Hitler's Europe, the section of a city where Jews were forced to live apart from other groups, in conditions of extreme crowding and deprivation.

Holocaust A term for the state-sponsored, systematic persecution and annihilation of European Jewry by Nazi Germany and its collaborators between 1933 and 1945. Millions of Jews and other people were murdered during that period.

Jews People who belong to the religion of Judaism.

Judenrat "Jewish Council," a group of Jews selected by the Germans to run the ghettos.

Judenrein "Purified of Jews," a German expression for Hitler's plan to rid Germany of all Jews.

Lebensraum A German term for "living space" outside of Germany to accommodate what the Nazis called the "master race" of Aryan people.

Liberation The freeing of the Nazis' victims from the death and concentration camps at the end of the war.

Liquidation The removal and murder of residents of the ghettos and the camps.

Nazi A member of the Nazi Party or something associated with the party, such as "Nazi government."

Nazi Party Short for the National Socialist German Workers' Party. Founded in 1919, the party became a potent political force under Hitler's leadership.

Nutzlos Esser Literally, "useless eaters," a term used by the Nazis to refer to the mentally and physically handicapped.

Palestine A region in the Middle East, part of which is now known as Israel. Palestine was controlled by the British government from 1922 to 1948.

Partisans Groups of independent fighters who lived in the woods or other remote areas and harassed the German Army or the SS in an effort to disrupt their actions.

Pogroms Organized, mass attacks on a group of people.

Propaganda The deliberate spreading of ideas, information or rumors—often false—for the purpose of helping or injuring a cause, organization, or person.

Resettlement A term used by the Nazis to make Jews believe that they were being transported to work camps in Eastern Europe, when in fact they were being taken to camps.

Resistance A general term for actions taken by individuals from various countries, both Jews and Gentiles, against the Nazis. Members of resistance groups worked "underground," in secrecy.

SS From the German term *Schutzstaffel,* meaning "defense unit." The SS began as Hitler's personal bodyguard and developed into the most powerful and feared organization in the Third Reich. *Also called black-shirts.*

Selection The process by which the Nazis determined which victims at the death camps would be spared to work and which ones would be killed immediately.

Sonderkommando A German word meaning "special detail." The term was used by the Nazis to refer to those prisoners in the death camp who were assigned to remove the bodies from the gas chambers and put them in the crematoria to be burned.

Star of David The six-pointed star that is a symbol of Judaism.

Third Reich *Reich* means "empire." In German history, the First Reich lasted from 962 until 1806, the second from 1871 to 1918. In the early 1920s, Hitler began using the term "Third Reich" to describe his own empire, which lasted from 1933 until 1945.

Untermenschen A German word meaning "subhumans," used by the Nazis to refer to some groups they considered "undesirable"—Jews, Romani, male homosexuals, political opponents, and the physically and mentally disabled.

Source Notes

Introduction:

Page 10: "Think of your mother. . . ." *Awake.* June 8, 1996, pp. 18–19.

Page 13: "Not all of the victims were Jewish. . . ." Barbara Rogasky. *Smoke and Ashes.* New York: Holiday House, 1988, p. 5.

Chapter 1:

Page 15: "I spent four days. . . ." Anton Gill. *The Journey Back From Hell.* New York: William Morrow & Co., 1988, p. 278.

Page 16: "Executions were carried out. . . ." Martin Gilbert. *Atlas of the Holocaust.* Oxford, England: Pergamon Press, 1988, p. 160.

Page 17: "We knew that we would be the first to fall. . . ." Leni Yahil. *The Holocaust: The Fate of European Jewry.* New York: Oxford University Press, 1990, p. 471.

Page 18: ". . . human beings had pedigrees. . . ." Simon Wiesenthal. *The Murderers Among Us.* New York: McGraw-Hill Book Company, 1967, p. 157.

Page 18: "[He] was a doctor." David A. Adler. *We Remember the Holocaust.* New York: Henry Holt and Company, 1989, p. 82.

Page 19: "At Majdanek. . . ." Konnilyn Feig. *Hitler's Death Camps.* New York: Holmes & Meier, 1979, p. 313.

Page 19: "At this place. . . ." Feig, p. 284.

Page 22–23: "They took me away. . . ." Jean-Francois Steiner. *Treblinka.* New York: Simon and Schuster, 1967, pp. 86-87.

Page 23: "Finding Jews. . . ." Carol Rittner and Sondra Myers, eds. *The Courage to Care.* New York: New York University Press, 1986, pp. 87–88.

Page 23: "Jews don't owe us gratitude. . . ." Rittner and Myers, p. 89.

Chapter 2:

Page 26: "They weren't about to wait. . . ." Identification Card #3962. Washington, D.C.: United States Holocaust Memorial Museum.

Page 27: ". . . That evening the children. . . ." Primo Levi. *Survival in Auschwitz and the Reawakening: Two Memoirs.* New York: Summit Books, 1986, pp. 6–7.

Page 28: "[The train] was so crowded. . . ." Adler, p. 69.

Page 28: "We can talk...." Noakes and Pridham, eds. *Nazism 1919–1945.* Vol. 3, *Foreign Policy, War and Racial Extermination.* Exeter, England: University of Exeter Press, p. 1199.

Page 30: "Everything movable. . . ." Zdenka Novak. *When Heaven's Vault Cracked.* Braunton, Devon, England: Merlin Books, 1995, pp. 47–48.

Page 32: "First, the guards herded the Jews. . . ." Feig, p. 321.

Page 32: "A transfer to Auschwitz. . . ." Feig, p. 323.

Page 33: "The 'wash barrack'...." Helen Waterford. *Commitment to the Dead.* Frederick, CO: Renaissance House Publishers, 1987, p. 66.

Page 33: "He spoke quietly. . . ." Elie Wiesel. *Night.* New York: Bantam Books, 1960, p. 71.

Chapter 3:

Page 35: "In some places. . . ." Feig, p. 330.

Page 40: "...an ideal suburban community. . . ." Feig, p. 257.

Page 40: "The Jewish children. . . ." Feig, p. 249.

Page 41: "We got used to sleeping without. . . ." Hana Volavkova and the United States Holocaust Memorial Council. *I Never Saw Another Butterfly.* New York: Schocken Books, 1993, p. 6.

Page 41: "For seven weeks. . . ." Volavkova and the Council, p. 39.

Chapter 4:

Page 43: "...exterminate the vermin. . . ." John Toland. *Adolf Hitler, Vol. 2.* New York: Doubleday & Co., 1976, p. 863.

Page 44: "We didn't know. . . ." Margaret Bourke-White. *Portrait of Myself.* New York: Simon & Schuster, 1963, pp. 258–259.

Page 44: "When their hearts spoke. . . ." Rittner & Myers, p. 99.

Page 44: "Those of us who received. . . ." Bourke-White, pp. 102, 107.

Page 45: "The women and children. . . ." Gilbert, p. 195.

Page 47: "Life is difficult. . . ." Nechama Tec. *Defiance: The Bielski Partisans.* New York: Oxford University Press, Inc., 1993, dust jacket, back flap.

Page 48: ". . . that it was more important. . . ." Tec, dust jacket, front flap.

Page 50: ". . . to have every chance. . . ." Waterford, p. 34.

Page 50: "They looked through our few belongings. . . ." Waterford, p. 53.

Page 50: "If [the other people] knew about...." Waterford, p. 54.
Page 51: "Rumors about the destination...." Waterford, p. 55.

Chapter 5:
Pages 53–54: "They, too, had been arrested...." Waterford, pp. 59–60.
Page 55: "He came right out...." Claude Lanzmann. *Shoah: An Oral History of the Holocaust.* New York: Pantheon Books, 1985, p. 126.
Page 57: "Three hundred women...." Waterford, p. 70.
Page 59: "Anything that looked like...." Michael Berenbaum. *The World Must Know.* Boston: Little, Brown, 1993, p. 165.
Page 59: "I do not know...." Berenbaum, p. 166.
Page 60: "The children's camp group...." Berenbaum, pp. 182–183.

Chapter 6:
Page 64: "[But] for most of it...." Berenbaum, p. 9.
Page 65: "We were tormented with hunger...." Wiesel, pp. 108–109.
Page 65: "From the depths of the mirror..." Wiesel, p. 109.
Page 66: "The cruel and universal weapon...." Lambert and Bow. *The Holocaust.* [A compact disc.] Minneapolis: Quanta Press Inc., 1994. "Interview with Congressman Dewey Short"
Page 66: "Buchenwald was more than the mind...." Bourke-White, pp. 258–259.
Page 67: "...combed-out and cut off...." Berenbaum, p. 149.
Page 69: "We saw enormous covered...." Feig, pp. 370–371.
Page 70: "Some of the photographs...." Gilbert, p. 230.
Page 71: "Between 1941 and 1944...." Pola Jasphy. *The Hidden Child.* Winter 1994. New York: The Hidden Child Foundation/ADL, p. 2.
Page 71: "Unbelief, nausea, repulsion...." Lambert and Bow.
Page 72: "As I approached them...." Gilbert, p. 227.
Page 72: "...during the years of struggle...." George H. Stein. *Hitler: Great Lives Observed.* Englewood Cliffs, NJ: Prentice-Hall, 1968, p. 83.

Bibliography

David Adler. *We Remember the Holocaust.* New York: Henry Holt and Company, 1989.
Awake. Newsletter, June 8, 1996.
Eleanor H. Ayer. *The United States Holocaust Memorial Museum: America Keeps the Memory Alive.* New York: Macmillan Publishing, 1994.
Eleanor Ayer. *Parallel Journeys.* New York: Atheneum, 1995.
Eleanor Ayer. *The Importance of Adolf Hitler.* San Diego: Lucent Books, 1996.
Michael Berenbaum. *The World Must Know.* Boston: Little, Brown, 1993.
Margaret Bourke-White. *Portrait of Myself.* New York: Simon & Schuster, 1963.
Konnilyn Feig. *Hitler's Death Camps.* New York: Holmes & Meier, 1979.
Martin Gilbert. *Atlas of the Holocaust.* Oxford, England: Pergamon Press, 1988.
Anton Gill. *The Journey Back From Hell.* New York: William Morrow & Co., 1988.
Mania Halevi. *Give Me Shelter For the Night.* (Unpublished manuscript)
The Hidden Child. Newsletter. Winter 1994. New York: The Hidden Child Foundation/Anti Defamation League.
Identification Card #3962. Washington, D.C.: United States Holocaust Memorial Museum.
Lambert and Bow. *The Holocaust.* [A compact disc.] Minneapolis: Quanta Press Inc., 1994.
Claude Lanzmann. *Shoah: An Oral History of the Holocaust.* New York: Pantheon Books, 1985.
Primo Levi. *If This Is a Man.* New York: Summit Books, no date.
Zdenka Novak. *When Heaven's Vault Cracked.* Braunton, Devon, England: Merlin Books, 1995.
Carol Rittner and Sondra Myers, editors. *The Courage to Care.* New York: New York University Press, 1986.
Barbara Rogasky. *Smoke and Ashes.* New York: Holiday House, 1988.
George H. Stein. *Hitler: Great Lives Observed.* Englewood Cliffs, NJ: Prentice-Hall, 1968.
Jean-Francois Steiner. *Treblinka.* New York: Simon & Schuster, 1967.
Nechama Tec. *Defiance: The Bielski Partisans.* New York: Oxford University Press, Inc., 1993.
John Tolland. *Adolf Hitler.* Volume 2. New York: Doubleday, 1976.
Hana Volavkova and the United States Holocaust Memorial Council. *I Never Saw Another Butterfly.* New York: Schocken Books, 1993.
Helen Waterford. *Commitment to the Dead.* Frederick, CO: Renaissance House Publishers, 1987.
Elie Wiesel. *Night.* New York: Bantam Books, 1960.
Simon Wiesenthal. *The Murderers Among Us.* New York: McGraw-Hill, 1967.
Leni Yahil. *The Holocaust: The Fate of European Jewry.* New York: Oxford University Press, 1990.

Further Reading

David Adler. *We Remember the Holocaust.* New York: Henry Holt and Company, 1989.
Eleanor H. Ayer. *The United States Holocaust Memorial Museum: America Keeps the Memory Alive.* New York: Macmillan Publishing, 1994.
Eleanor H. Ayer. *Parallel Journeys.* New York: Antheneum, 1995.
Eleanor H. Ayer. *The Importance of Adolf Hitler.* San Diego: Lucent Books, 1996.
Michael Berenbaum. *The World Must Know.* Boston: Little, Brown, 1993.
Anne Frank. *The Diary of a Young Girl.* The Definitive Edition. New York: Doubleday, 1995.
Martin Gilbert. *Atlas of the Holocaust.* Oxford, England: Pergamon Press, 1988.
Lambert and Bow. *The Holocaust.* A compact disc. Minneapolis: Quanta Press, Inc., 1994.
Claude Lanzmann. *Shoah: An Oral History of the Holocaust.* New York: Pantheon Books, 1985.
Lois Lowry, *Number the Stars.* New York: Dell Publishing, 1990.
Carol Rittner and Sondra Myers, editors. *The Courage to Care.* New York: New York University Press, 1986.
Barbara Rogasky. *Smoke and Ashes.* New York: Holiday House, 1988.
Hana Volavkova and the United States Holocaust Memorial Council. *I Never Saw Another Butterfly.* New York: Schocken Books, 1993.
Elie Wiesel. *Night.* New York: Bantam Books, 1960.
Leni Yahil. *The Rescue of Danish Jewry: Test of a Democracy.* New York: The Jewish Publication Society, 1969.

Index

A

Allied forces, 44–46, **45**, 63
"Angel of Death." *See* Mengele, Josef
Artz, Louis, 10
Auschwitz–Birkenau concentration camp, **52**
  evacuation of, 60–61
  liberation of, 60–61
  overview of, 18–19
  revolt at, 55–56

B

Belzec death camp, 19
Berenbaum, Michael, 59
Bergen-Belsen concentration camp, 68–69
Bernstein, Cecilia, 27–28
Bialystok Ghetto revolt, 17
Bielski, Tuvia, 47–48
Birkenau death camp. *See* Auschwitz–Birkenau concentration camp
Black-shirts
  control over Hungary, 36
  overthrowing of at Auschwitz–Birkenau, 56
Blatt, Tomasz, 25–26
Bourke-White, Margaret, 44, 66
Braun, Eva, 72
Buchenwald concentration camp, **8**, **21**, 64–66
Buergenthal, Thomas, 60–61
Buna-Monowitz labor camp, 18

C

Chasid, Joseph and Rachel, **38**
Chelmno death camp, 19, 60
Children, persecution of, 39–41, 49, **52**, 54, 70
Chronology of Holocaust, 73
Churchill, Winston, 63
Concentration camps
  Auschwitz–Birkenau, 18–19, **52**, 55–56, 60–61
  Bergen-Belsen, 68–69
  Buchenwald, **8**, **21**, 64–66
  Dachau, **21**, **68**, 70
  general description of, 66
  liberation of, 60–61, 63–66, 65 (map), **68**, 69–70
  listing/descriptions of largest, 20–21
  locations of, 17 (map)
  Ohrdruf, 63–64
  Ravensbrück, 71–72
  Theresienstadt, 40
  See also Death camps
Cracow ghetto, 31
Cremation, 55, 61

D

Dachau concentration camp, **21**, **68**, 70
Danish Jews, 23
D-Day, 44–46
Death camps
  Auschwitz–Birkenau, 18–19, **52**, 55–56, 60–61
  Belzec, 19
  Chelmno, 19, 60
  locations of, 17 (map)
  Majdanek, 19, 32
  Sobibór, 19, 25–26
  Treblinka, 22
  See also concentration camps
Death counts, Jewish, 69 (chart)
Death marches, **42**, 51 (map), 57, 60–61
Deportations
  increase of, **12**, 16 (map), 16–17, 36–37, 46–47, 49, 51 (map)
  train conditions, 27–28
Detention camps, 27

E

Eichmann, Adolf, 36–37
Eisenhower, Dwight D., **62**, 63, 66
Epidemic, typhus, 68–70
Escape attempts, Jewish. *See* resistance groups
Experiments, medical, 18
Extermination camps. *See* death camps

F

Feig, Konnilyn, 19, 40
Fischl, Petr, 40–41
Foreign reaction to Jewish massacre, 13
Frank, Anne, 53, 57
Frank, Edith and Margot, 57
Frank, Hans, **16**

G

Gassing of Jews, 19, 22, 49, 54–55, 58
Genocide, 10
Gentiles. *See* Non-Jews
Germany
  allied invasions of Europe, 44–46, 63
  domination in Europe, 11 (map)
  invasion of neighboring countries, 9, 36
  Italy declares war on, 26–28
  public reaction to Nazi atrocities, 44, 67
  surrender in World War II, 72
Gestapo, 10, 15
Ghettos, Jewish, 16–17, 31
Gilbert, Martin, 16, 45, 71
Graves, mass, 16, 60
Greek Jews, persecution of, 37, **38**, 39

H

Hidden Child Foundation, 70
Himmler, Heinrich, 10, **16**, 22, 26, 28, 49, 58
  See also SS (*Schutzstaffel*)
Hitler, Adolf, 9, 36, **56**
  assassination plots against, 48
  decline of power, 63
  suicide of, 72
  view of Jewish "race," 43
  See also Nazi Party; Nazis
Hizme, Irene, 18
Holocaust
  chronology of, 73
  definition of, 10–11
Hungarian Jews, 36–37, 59

I

I Never Saw Another Butterfly (Fischl), 40–41
Irgun Brit Zion (ABZ), **29**
Italian war on Germany, 26–28

J

Jasphy, Pola, 70–71
Jews
  cremation of, 55, 61
  death counts, 69 (chart)
  deportation of, **12**, 16–17, 36–37, 46–47, 49, 51
  extermination of, 36–37, 39, 45, 59
  gassing of, 19, 22, 49, 54–55, 58
  medical experiments on, 18
Judenrat, 36–37

K

Keneally, Thomas, 31
Kieler, Jørgen, 23
Killing centers. *See* death camps

L

Labor camps. *See* concentration camps
Levi, Primo, 27

M

Majdanek death camp, 19, 32
Medical experiments performed on Jews, 18

Mengele, Josef, 18, 54
Müller, Filip, 55
Murrow, Edward, 64
Mussolini, Benito, 26

N
National Socialist German Workers' Party. *See* Nazi Party
Nazi Party
 collaborators, **57**
 decline of power, 63, 72
 rise to power, 10
 use of propaganda, 40
 See also Hitler, Adolf
Nazis
 deportation of Jews, 28, 46, 49, 51
 German public reaction to, 13, 67
 invasion of neighboring countries, 9, 36
 killing of French Jews, 45
 murder of non-Jews, 19
 resistance groups against, 16–17, 23, 25–26, 28–30, 47–50, 55–58, 60
 See also Hitler, Adolf
Non-Jews
 deaths of, 19
 reluctance to help Jews, 43–44
Novak, Zdenka, 28–30

O
Ohrdruf concentration camp, 63–64
Operation Barbarossa, 43

P
Partisan groups. *See* resistance groups
Patton, George, 64, 66–67
Propaganda about concentration camps, 40

R
Ravensbrück women's camp, 71–72
Red Cross visit to Theresienstadt concentration camp, 40
Resettlement of Jews. *See* deportations
Resistance groups, 16–17, 23, 25–26, 28–30, **29**, 47–50, **48**, 55–58, 60
 location of uprisings, 51 (map)
Revolts, Jewish. *See* resistance groups
Roosevelt, Franklin D., 13
Rosenthal, Avram and Emmanuel, **24**

S
Sauvage, Pierre, 44
Schindler, Oskar, **31**
Schindler's List (Keneally), 31
Short, Dewey, 66
Slotkin, Rene, 18
Sobibór death camp, 19, 25–26
Sonderkommando revolt, 55–58, 60
Soviet Army, 58, 60–61
"Special Detail" revolt, 55–58, 60
SS (*Schutzstaffel*)
 control over Hungary, 36
 overthrowing of at Auschwitz–Birkenau, 56
 role of, 10
Stauffenberg, Claus, 48
Stobierski, Mieczyslaw, 61
Survival in Auschwitz (Levi), 27
Survivors, legacy of, 70–71

T
Theresienstadt concentration camp, **39**, 40
Trains, deportation, 27–28
Transit camps, 27
Treblinka death camp, 22
Trocme, Andre and Magda, 44
Typhus, 68–70

U
Underground defense groups. *See* resistance groups
Unger, Aviva, 15–16
United States
 Holocaust Memorial Museum, 35, 61
 reaction to Nazism, 13
Untermenschen, 9–10
Uprisings, 16–17, 22–23, 25–26, 51 (map), 55–58

W
Wallenberg, Raoul, **59**
Wiesel, Elie, 13, 64–65
Wiesenthal, Simon, 18
Williams, Lyle, 71
Wohlfarth, Doris, Helen, and Siegfried, 50–51, 53–54, 57
World War II
 allied invasion of Europe, 44–46, 63
 ending of, 72

Y
Yochai, Boris, **30**

Poem, page 41: From *I Never Saw Another Butterfly, Expanded 2nd Edition* by U.S. Holocaust Memorial Council, edited by Hana Volavkova. ©1978, 1993 by Artia, Prague. Compilation ©1993 by Schocken Books Inc. Reprinted by permission of Schocken Books, distributed by Pantheon Books, a division of Random House, Inc.

Photo Credits

Cover and pages 52, 53: State Archives of the Russian Federation, courtesy of USHMM Photo Archives; pages 8, 9: David Wherry, courtesy of USHMM Photo Archives; pages 12, 14, 15, 71: Main Commission for the Investigation of Nazi War Crimes, courtesy of USHMM Photo Archives; page 16: Museum of the History of Photography, courtesy of USHMM Photo Archives; pages 20, 45, 54, 56, 62, 63, 67: National Archives; pages 21 (top), 57, 64, 68: National Archives, courtesy of USHMM Photo Archives; page 21 (bottom): Frances Robert Arzt, courtesy of USHMM Photo Archives; page 22: Frihedsmuseet, courtesy of USHMM Photo Archives; pages 24, 25: George Kadish, courtesy of USHMM Photo Archives; page 29: Sara Trozki Koper, courtesy of USHMM Photo Archives; page 30: YIVO Institute for Jewish Research, courtesy of USHMM Photo Archives; page 31: Prof. Leopold Pfefferberg-Page, courtesy of USHMM Photo Archives; page 38: Courtesy of USHMM Photo Archives; pages 34, 35: Ivan Vojtech Fric, courtesy of USHMM Photo Archives; page 36: National Archives: Suitland, courtesy of USHMM Photo Archives; page 39: Yad Vashem Photo Archives, courtesy of USHMM Photo Archives; pages 42, 43: KZ Gedenkstatte Dachau, courtesy of USHMM Photo Archives; page 47: Henri Krischer, courtesy of USHMM Photo Archives; page 48: TASS, courtesy of USHMM Photo Archives; page 49: Ghetto Fighters' House, courtesy of USHMM Photo Archives; page 58: Central Armed Forces, courtesy of USHMM Photo Archives; page 59: on loan from the Wallenberg family to USHMM.

All maps and graphs ©Blackbirch Press, Inc.

Gloucester Library
P.O. Box 2380
Gloucester, VA 23061

DATE DUE

JUN 9 '98			
FEB 20 '99			
APR 18 '99			

GL

j940.53
18 Ayer, Eleanor H.
Aye Inferno

$18.95 3/98

Gloucester Library
P.O. Box
Gloucester, VA 23061